WHITE FOLKS

White Folks explores the experiences and stories of eight white people from a small farming community in northern Wisconsin. It examines how white people learn to be 'white' and reveals how white racial identity is dependent on people of color—even in situations where white people have little or no contact with racial others.

Drawing on in-depth interviews with Delores, Frank, William, Erin, Robert, Libby, and Stan, as well as on his own experiences growing up in this same rural community, Lensmire creates a portrait of white people that highlights how their relations to people of color and their cultures are seldom simple and are characterized not just by fear and rejection, but also by attraction, envy, and desire. *White Folks* helps readers recognize the *profound ambivalence* that has characterized white thinking and feeling in relation to people of color for at least the last two hundred years. There is nothing smooth about the souls of white folks.

Current antiracist work is often grounded in a white privilege framework that has proven ineffective—in part because it reduces white people to little more than the embodiment of privilege. Lensmire provides an alternative that confronts the violence at the core of white racial selves that has become increasingly visible in American society and politics, but that also illuminates conflicts and complexities there.

Timothy J. Lensmire is Professor in the Department of Curriculum and Instruction at the University of Minnesota, where he teaches courses in literacy, critical pedagogy, and race. His early work focused on how the teaching of writing might contribute to education for radical democracy. His current research seeks to build descriptions of, and theoretical insights about, how white people learn to be white in a white supremacist society.

Writing Lives
Ethnographic Narratives
Series Editors: Arthur P. Bochner, Carolyn Ellis and Tony E. Adams
University of South Florida and Northeastern Illinois University

Writing Lives: Ethnographic Narratives publishes narrative representations of qualitative research projects. The series editors seek manuscripts that blur the boundaries between humanities and social sciences. We encourage novel and evocative forms of expressing concrete lived experience, including auto-ethnographic, literary, poetic, artistic, visual, performative, critical, multi-voiced, conversational, and co-constructed representations. We are interested in ethnographic narratives that depict local stories; employ literary modes of scene setting, dialogue, character development, and unfolding action; and include the author's critical reflections on the research and writing process, such as research ethics, alternative modes of inquiry and representation, reflexivity, and evocative storytelling. Proposals and manuscripts should be directed to abochner@usf.edu, cellis@usf.edu or aeadams3@neiu.edu

Other volumes in this series include:

Evocative Autoethnography
Writing Lives and Telling Stories
Arthur P. Bochner and Carolyn Ellis

Bullied
Tales of Torment, Identity, and Youth
Keith Berry

Collaborative and Indigenous Mental Health Therapy
Tātaihono – Stories of Maori Healing and Psychiatry
Wiremu NiaNia, Allister Bush and David Epston

Searching for an Autoethnographic Ethic
Stephen Andrew

Autobiography of a Disease
Patrick Anderson

For a full list of titles in this series, please visit:
https://www.routledge.com/Writing-Lives-Ethnographic-Narratives/book-series/WLEN

WHITE FOLKS

Race and Identity in Rural America

Timothy J. Lensmire

Routledge
Taylor & Francis Group

NEW YORK AND LONDON

First published 2017
by Routledge
711 Third Avenue, New York, NY 10017

and by Routledge
2 Park Square, Milton Park, Abingdon, Oxon, OX14 4RN

Routledge is an imprint of the Taylor & Francis Group, an informa business

© 2017 Taylor & Francis

Library of Congress Cataloging-in-Publication Data
Names: Lensmire, Timothy J., 1961- author.
Title: White folks : race and identity in rural America / Timothy J. Lensmire.
Description: New York, NY : Routledge, 2017. | Series: Writing lives : ethnographic narratives
Identifiers: LCCN 2017001423| ISBN 9781138747012 (hardback) | ISBN 9781138747036 (paperback) | ISBN 9781315180359 (ebook)
Subjects: LCSH: Whites--Race identity--United States. | Racism--United States. | United States--Race relations. | United States--Rural conditions. | Whites--Wisconsin--Interviews. | Ethnology--Wisconsin. | Lensmire, Timothy J., 1961---Childhood and youth. | Wisconsin--Biography. | Wisconsin--Race relations. | Wisconsin--Rural conditions.
Classification: LCC E184.A1 L4446 2017 | DDC 305.800973--dc23
LC record available at https://lccn.loc.gov/2017001423

ISBN: 978-1-138-74701-2 (hbk)
ISBN: 978-1-138-74703-6 (pbk)
ISBN: 978-1-315-18035-9 (ebk)

Typeset in Bembo
by Saxon Graphics Ltd, Derby

To my passionate, brilliant, and ridiculous children—John, Sarah, Isabelle, and Jacob—and to my parents, Lynn and John Lensmire (who are all those things, too)

CONTENTS

ACKNOWLEDGMENTS

I relied on the intellectual and emotional support of a number of friends and colleagues at the University of Minnesota as I worked on this book. Thank you, especially, to Vichet Chhuon, Cynthia Lewis, Bic Ngo, Thom Swiss, Mark Vagle, and Martha Bigelow. I also want to acknowledge James Ysseldkye, the late Ruth Thomas, and Deborah Dillon, who in their administrative roles provided support for my initial research and writing.

I have been fortunate to be part of the Midwest Critical Whiteness Collective. For the last seven years, we have been telling stories to each other and trying to figure out what they mean—thank you to Audrey Lensmire, Zachary Casey, Mary Lee-Nichols, Shannon McManimon, Bryan Davis, Jessica Tierney, Sam Tanner, and Christina Berchini. Thanks also to Nathan Snaza, Jim Jupp, and Erin Miller for what I've learned writing with you; to John Wright for help with Ralph Ellison; and to Patty Loew for early conversations on the history of the Ojibwe in Wisconsin.

Some conversations stretch over decades, constitute you, continue whether or not the other person happens to be with you at the moment. I'm grateful to Jim Garrison and Garrett Duncan for these. And to Emmanuel Harris II, my brother.

Finally, it's nice living with a sophisticated race theorist when you are trying to write a book like this. But I am thankful to Audrey Lensmire for more than reading my work, commenting, encouraging, and reading some more. We write and teach and holler and laugh. I am grateful for the very life we live together.

The author expresses his appreciation for permission to adapt and reprint his previously published material in the following chapters:

Chapter 1 includes a revised version of an article published in 2008, "How I became white while punching de tar baby," *Curriculum Inquiry, 38*(3), 299–322.

Chapter 2 includes a revised version of "Ambivalent white racial identities: Fear and an elusive innocence," *Race Ethnicity and Education, 13*(2) (2010), 159–172, published by Taylor and Francis; and a revised version of an article published in 2011, "Laughing white men," in *Journal of Curriculum Theorizing, 27*(3), 102–116.

Chapter 3 is a revised version of "White men's racial others," *Teachers College Record, 116*(3) (2014), 1–32, www.tcrecord.org/content.asp?contentid=17357.

Chapter 4 includes material from an article published in 2013, "Dirt and early reading," *Bankstreet Occasional Papers Series, 29*, https://www.bankstreet.edu/occasional-paper-series/29/dirt-and-early-reading/.

THE FORETHOUGHT

They were waiting for muskrat to come back.

The Creator, Gitchi Manito, had flooded the entire Earth. Waynaboozhoo[1] and the animals took turns resting on a giant log.

Waynaboozhoo thought that, with a bit of Earth, and with the help of the Four Winds and Gitchi Manito, they could create new land on which to live.

So Waynaboozhoo, then the loon, the helldiver, the mink, and the turtle, had dived deep into the water to bring back some Earth. But they had all failed. The water was too deep and they each had returned to the surface, in turn, gasping for breath. Then the muskrat said that he would try.

He was gone too long. When he floated to the surface, drowned, Waynaboozhoo and the animals began a song of mourning. But their song was interrupted when Waynaboozhoo realized that little muskrat had made it to the bottom and, even in death, had brought a piece of Earth with him, in his paw, to the surface.

Waynaboozhoo put the bit of Earth on the turtle's back. The Four Winds blew. The ball of Earth grew and grew, became a huge island, the new Earth.

★   ★   ★

Gitchi Manito—with Waynaboozhoo, the Seven Grandfathers, and the teachings and prophecies of the Seven Fires—helped and guided the Anishinabe as they lived and prospered in the new Earth.

One of the Seven Fires directed the people to their chosen ground, a "land where food grows on water" (*Manoomin*, wild rice). Moningwunakawning, later renamed Madeline Island by the Ojibwe, became the spiritual and economic center of the Ojibwe nation, which included most of what is now northern Wisconsin and parts of Minnesota and Michigan's Upper Peninsula.

Another of the prophecies of the Seven Fires foretold the coming of the Light-skinned Race and cautioned the people to take care, as it would be difficult to tell if the newcomers wore the face of *neekonnisiwin* (brotherhood) or *niboowin* (death).

The Light-skinned Race did come, and for many years, it appeared that the Ojibwe and the French were creating bonds of affection and brotherhood that would last. The Ojibwe assimilated the French into their families and communities, encouraged intermarriage, and fought alongside their friends and kin against the English as hostilities between France and England edged closer to their home.

★　　★　　★

The Light-skinned Race did come, and in the end, it wore the face of death.

President Andrew Jackson, in 1830, signed the Indian Removal Act, which claimed that the United States had the right to forcibly remove tribes from their homelands east of the Mississippi River. In treaties with the United States in 1837 and 1842 and 1854, the Ojibwe were forced to give up millions of acres of land—millions of acres of land that, if reckoned in terms of the Light-skinned Race, could be turned into 170 billion board feet of timber and 150 billion tons of iron ore.

The people's leaders insisted in these treaties on the right to hunt and fish and gather on the land they had given up. Four reservations were created in Wisconsin that, of the original millions, totaled 275,000 acres.

★　　★　　★

They despaired of the future, these working people of Pittsburgh, the Smoky City. When the women weren't working in the needle trades or cleaning rich people's houses, they were trying to keep their families' small rooms in the tenement houses clean—in neighborhoods with no running water or sewers, in neighborhoods getting dirtier and more densely populated by the day. In the foundries, wages declined and working conditions deteriorated, as owners cut costs to corner the national market in iron. The men worked at piecework their 70 or so hours a week, when they weren't laid off for weeks at a time.

In 1856, a small group of these working people formed the Pittsburgh German Settlers Club. They bought 3,000 acres of what had been taken from the Ojibwe. The ones that didn't give up and go back East stayed and labored to clear the land of timber. The land they cleared, they farmed. The Town of Boonendam was formed.

★　　★　　★

Soon enough, they had Polish neighbors. They came to the United States from occupied Poland, after the Franco-Prussian War. They fled poverty and new restrictions on their Polish language and Catholic Church—punishments for Polish support of France in the War; punishments (let's be honest) for being Polish.

They arrived in Milwaukee in time for the Long Depression (1873–1879). In 1875, despairing of the future, they bought, next to Boonendam, some of what had been taken from the Ojibwe.

They thought it a fine joke (by God? that they played on themselves?) that they had fled the Germans in Prussia and now found themselves attending a German Catholic church on Sundays and, the rest of the week, buying provisions from German shopkeepers. They would eventually build their own Polish Catholic church, but at least these Germans of Boonendam, Wisconsin, spoke more German than they did English. German might stick in their throats, but these Poles of Boonendam, Wisconsin, could speak it better than the new language of America.

★   ★   ★

These Germans and Poles became American. They became white. Boonendam grew, but never to much more than a thousand people in town and another two or three thousand in the surrounding countryside. There was a Catholic elementary school, named Blessed Virgin, and a public elementary school, too (for the Lutherans). Then, the children all went to the public high school, together, where youthful attraction and desire helped erode older divisions of nationality and religion.

Impose whatever images or storylines onto this small town and its people that you must. Rural, isolated—yes. Always already dreaming the nation's dreams of democracy and progress and white supremacy (and haunted by its nightmares); always already vulnerable to the demands of capital—yes. Like many in the state and nation, these white people were surprised and angered when a hundred or so years after the founding of Boonendam on land taken from the Ojibwe, *real people*—rather than the make-believe Indians they dressed their children as for Thanksgiving programs at school or the blood-thirsty caricatures they encountered in novels and movies—real people claimed treaty rights to hunt and fish on ceded Ojibwe territory and occupied the Northern States Power Company dam, near Hayward, Wisconsin, in protest of the flooding of their wild rice beds 50 years before. Like many white people in the United States, they looked on in puzzlement and fear as *real people*—rather than the comic Sambo or violent black criminal stereotypes they knew from blackface minstrelsy shows and newspapers and radio and TV—real people demanded equality and civil rights from a nation these white people pretended was already fair and true.

★   ★   ★

And, finally, need I add that I who speak here am bone of the bone and flesh of the flesh of them that lived and dreamed white America in Boonendam, Wisconsin?

Note

1 Waynaboozhoo was a spirit with human-like characteristics who had many adventures during the early years of the Earth. My account of the creation of a new Earth and other parts of this forethought are based on Edward Benton-Banai's (1988) *The Mishomis Book: The Voice of the Ojibway*. I have also drawn on Patty Loew's (2001) *Indian Nations of Wisconsin: Histories of Endurance and Renewal*. I am a white writer appropriating these two Ojibwe writers' work for my own purposes, so you should not trust my retellings of their stories here—go read their books for yourself. This is necessary even as a primary goal in retelling these stories is to disrupt, to *oppose*, the white supremacist assumption that the story of a place starts when white people get there.

1

HOW I BECAME WHITE WHILE PUNCHING DE TAR BABY

Call me Timothy.[1]

When I was young—never mind how long ago precisely—my mother and father avoided direct talk about sex and aroused bodies with the phrase 'making love,' which they told me meant kissing and hugging (at the time, they did not tell me what else it could mean). When I was older, I remember laughing at myself as I watched a movie and I realized that when the scene faded to black with the passionate couple kissing and groping, my imagination just faded too—I assumed, somehow, that that was all. I did not keep the story going forward through the blackout, imagining what came next, even though, by this time, I knew what came next. My parents' use of 'making love' had left all this fuzzy and hidden, and I carried this forward with me even as I achieved greater understanding of making love elsewhere, at other times.

More recently, I realized that there was a similar disjuncture between what I knew and *what I knew* in relation to the word 'lynch.' I cannot and do not trace this strange knowing and not knowing to my parents—my guess is that the fade-out of my understanding and clarity was accomplished by textbooks and stories and movies with their vagueness and omissions. Or maybe it was just a wishing-it-were-otherwise within me. But I realized that I was somehow holding onto the belief that *lynch* didn't necessarily mean *kill*, even as I was reading *Southern Horrors: Lynch Law in All its Phases*, journalist Ida B. Wells's investigative work from the late 1800s on how lynching was used to terrorize and eliminate black people who were competing, economically, with white people (see Jones Royster, 1997). Finding Michael Fedo's (2000) book on the lynchings in 1920 in Duluth, Minnesota, in which three young black men were killed—and especially seeing a photo of the lynchings' result, a photo that later appeared on popular postcards commemorating the event for white people who couldn't be there in person (I am soul-sick)—this pushed me to the dictionary I have on my desk at home—"lynch: to put to death (as by hanging) by mob action without legal sanction". That is quite clear, like the photograph.

I have been trying to get smarter about how white people grow into and embody their whiteness, how we come to think and feel and act as we do. This book is the result of that effort. In this chapter, I use myself as an example—not because I am special, but because I am not. The lynchings in Duluth are not that far, in time or space, from where I grew up, in Boonendam, or from where I live now, in Minneapolis, Minnesota.[2]

In later chapters, I focus on the stories and experiences of seven other white people I interviewed from Boonendam. I think of them—Delores, Frank, William, Erin, Robert, Libby, and Stan—as my peers, from my home. We grew up in or near Boonendam and live there now (except for me). Our mothers farmed, worked in factories and their homes, were secretaries and teachers and nurses; our fathers drove tractor trailers, made cheese, farmed, worked in factories—one owned a small store in town. We, their children, became teachers and farmers, worked in factories and offices. White folks.

I asked them to try to remember the first time that they realized they were white and to narrate experiences in which race somehow mattered or was important. In the course of two, sometimes three, interviews, we sat for three or four or six hours and talked about how they thought the German and Polish origins of Boonendam influenced their lives there. We talked about how they and their community had responded to people of color in various situations and across different historical events, including the controversy surrounding Ojibwe efforts in the 1970s to claim fishing rights on nearby lakes and rivers and their interactions with recent arrivals to the area, especially Hmong and Mexican Americans hired to work on local farms.

I was born in 1961. Delores, the oldest of us, is a little more than a decade older than me; Frank, the youngest, about ten years younger. The rest are my age or close. As a group, we don't fit popular ways of parsing North American 'generations'—we straddle the baby boomer generation and Generation X.

A better way to locate us *in time*, then, is in relation to the social upheavals of the 1960s. Delores was in high school and then college during this time. At State College, where she was studying to be a teacher, Delores confronted—in a way none of the rest of us did—the question of whether or not she would participate actively in civil rights and antiwar protests. Her response to this question, which was to try to be an "innocent bystander," is explored in Chapter 2.

Frank, born in the early 1970s, grew up in the aftermath of the 1960s. I use his experiences and stories to help us understand how the civil rights movement taught white people that we weren't supposed to think and talk about people of color in the ways that we used to. Unfortunately, this did not mean that racist talk and thought and feeling disappeared. Instead, as Frank describes later in Chapter 2, it just went underground.

The rest of us grew up as the decade unfolded, too young and too far away from urban and university and Southern contexts to face, directly, Delores's dilemma of where and with whom to stand. And yet, as I explore in this chapter and Chapters 3 and 4, who we were as white people was amazingly dependent on real and imagined people of color. As white people, we *used* people of color to figure out who we were. We used, and continue to use, people of color to create ourselves as white Americans.

★   ★   ★

I did this, too—created my white self in relation to people of color. In the rest of this chapter, I return to a performance I did in high school. I told a story at a senior awards program, and my storytelling is best interpreted, I think, as latter-day blackface minstrelsy—one without blackface, but with a black folk tale and with ways of speaking and moving that my audience recognized as 'black.'[3]

I try to make sense of my performance's appeal to the rural community of my birth, and to make sense of what was at stake here for my white audience and me. I build up my interpretation in three layers: the first treats my performance as grounded in a rural sensibility and closeness to the land; the second explores how white working folk created a black 'other' who embodied what they longed for and despised; and the third recovers the hopeful early moves of blackface minstrelsy—moves later abandoned, perverted, in the pursuit of money and respectability.

Blackface minstrelsy emerged in the early 1830s and became the most popular form of entertainment in the United States in the nineteenth century. Cultural historian Eric Lott (1995), whose *Love and Theft* explores the relation of minstrelsy to the white American working class, notes that blackface minstrelsy was centered in the urban North and was a theatrical practice "organized around the quite explicit 'borrowing' of black cultural materials ... in which white men caricatured blacks for sport and profit" (p. 3). Although its form and content underwent revision over time, performances generally began with five white men on stage, arranged in a semicircle. The men had burnt cork or greasepaint applied as 'blackface' and were dressed in "outrageously oversized and/or ragged 'Negro' costumes" (p. 5). In the middle of the semicircle was Mr. Interlocutor, a sort of master of ceremonies, who used a less exaggerated version of counterfeit 'black dialect' and dressed more formally than his fellow performers. On either side of Mr. Interlocutor were musicians, most often banjo and violin players. On the ends of the semicircle were Mr. Tambo, the tambourine player, and Mr. Bones, with his bone castanets.

The show had three parts:

> The first part offered up a random selection of songs interspersed with what passed for black wit and japery; the second part (or "olio") featured a group

of novelty performances (comic dialogues, malapropistic "stump speeches," cross-dressed "wench" performances, and the like); and the third part was a narrative skit, usually set in the South, containing dancing, music, and burlesque.

(Lott, 1995, pp. 5–6)

As professional theater, blackface minstrelsy had largely disappeared by the 1920s. However, it lived on in countless amateur productions well into the 1960s. (In talking with my dad about this chapter, I learned that in the mid 1940s, my aunt had performed in blackface when her senior class had put on a minstrelsy show at Boonendam High.) Of course, even as minstrelsy-as-theater dwindled, performers and others continued to 'black up': in film, Al Jolson, Fred Astaire, Bing Crosby, and Betty Grable, among others, performed blackface numbers; in country music and vaudeville, blackface performers included Bill Monroe, Jimmie Rodgers, and Sophie Tucker; and white college fraternities, it seems, have a never-ending fondness for blackface in talent shows and Halloween parties.

For my purposes, it is not the presence or absence of minstrel shows or blackened white faces that is important. Lott (1995) argues that the minstrel show has been "so central to the lives of North Americans that we are hardly aware of its extraordinary influence," and that, consequently, "studying [minstrelsy] together with its characteristic audience is perhaps the *best way* to understand the affective life of the race in that time *and in ours*" (p. 4, my emphasis). For cultural critic and dance historian Brenda Dixon Gottschild (1996), what has "proven to be the most insidious level of minstrelization, from the Africanist perspective, is the way in which [its] influence has persisted in nonminstrel cultural forms"—specifically, how minstrelsy served to solidify and propagate the "minstrel stereotype as the true picture of black offstage life" (p. 124). Novelist and social critic Ralph Ellison (1953/1995) names this stereotype the "black mask"; historian Joseph Boskin (1986) calls it "Sambo." And, as Boskin documents in numbing detail, this minstrel stereotype is found everywhere, everywhen, in North American literature, film, radio, television, dance, and music.

It was this stereotype that I enacted in my high school performance. I told one of the Brer Rabbit stories, based on the tales published by white journalist Joel Chandler Harris in the late 1800s, first told to him, when he was a young man, by enslaved Africans on a Georgia plantation. Harris's Brer Rabbit stories have been controversial in the United States, but not because of the stories themselves. Instead, Harris's portrayal of the talk/dialect of slaves has drawn considerable criticism, as has his creation and use of a version of the minstrel stereotype—Uncle Remus—as narrator for the stories. My high school storytelling performance resuscitated Harris's creation. I told my story as Uncle Remus.

This chapter, then, is about the complex social production of white identity—in a small farming community, and in relation to books, teachers, schools, music, and movies. It is about becoming a self in community, about becoming a white person in a white community, and using black people and black cultural products to do it. If, as Italian political intellectual and activist Antonio Gramsci (1971) thought, the "starting point of critical elaboration is … 'knowing thyself' as a product of the historical process to date which has deposited in you an infinity of traces, without leaving an inventory" (p. 324), then I attempt, here, to elaborate not just my own historical process, but one many white people share. For the purpose, ultimately, of creating inventories, understanding traces, so that we might do critical and creative work with them, critical and creative work on our selves and our worlds.

★   ★   ★

It has happened three times in my life. The third was during a talk I gave at an education conference in San Francisco in the mid 1990s. The second, in the early '80s, when I was singing a solo in front of an overfull church on Easter Sunday. I noticed, as I began these performances, that I was losing any worry about how the audience would judge me and that, instead, I wanted acutely to serve, to care for my audience, in the performance. I lost my self in what felt sacred; I lost any cares save doing this well for them.

In relation to my life, these times stand out like that moment in *The Adventures of Huckleberry Finn* when Huck is watching two con men, the "duke" and the "king," deceive an entire community into believing that they are the long-lost brothers of someone recently deceased. In the midst of all this ridiculousness and falsity, something sacred happens. The king closes his little speech with what Mark Twain and Huck call a "pious goody-goody Amen," and then, Twain writes:

> And the minute the words were out of his mouth somebody over in the crowd struck up the doxolojer, and everybody joined in with all their might, and it just warmed you up and made you feel as good as church letting out. Music *is* a good thing; and after all that soul-butter and hogwash I never see it freshen up things so, and sound so honest and bully.
>
> *(1885/1962, p. 183)*

The first time was when I was a senior in high school. I participated in a series of speech contests that culminated in a competition in the state's capital, Madison, Wisconsin. I was a storyteller. I received first place at the state competition and was asked to perform my state-winning story at the awards program in the high school auditorium in late spring. That was the first time.

In Boonendam when I was growing up, the high school, with its athletics and plays and music, often served as the cultural center of the town. On the night of the awards program, the auditorium was filled and hot, and toward the end I told my story.

As I said, it felt sacred as I performed for my community. People laughed and clapped and cheered. Afterward, farmers who hauled milk to the small cheese factory run by my dad and my uncle (and earlier, by my grandfather) slapped me hard on the back, laughed, seemed almost to cut me with their dry, calloused skin as they smiled and shook my hand.

I can still remember my first lines:

> Way down south, in a deep dark forest, lived a little smarty-pants bunny. His name?

> Brer Rabbit.[4]

The story I told was "De Tar Baby," in which Brer Rabbit's enemies, Brer Fox and Brer Bear, make a small figure out of tar and then set their Tar Baby trap at the side of the road. The Tar Baby eventually enrages Brer Rabbit when it sits silent to Brer Rabbit's friendly greetings.

> "Howdy-do!" sing out Brer Rabbit.

> Of course, de Tar Baby, he say nothin'. Brer Rabbit wait. Den he say, louder than before, "Ain't you goin' to be perlite an say Howdy-do?"

> De Tar Baby, he say nothin'.

Brer Rabbit punches the Tar Baby, becoming stuck in Brer Fox and Brer Bear's trap. Of course, Brer Rabbit ultimately escapes, tricking his enemies by begging them to kill him in any horrible way possible, except, he begs them, except by throwing him into the briar patch.

> "Skin me," say Brer Rabbit, "pull out my ears, snatch off my legs, an chop off my tail, but please, *please*, PLEASE, Brer Fox an' Brer Bear, don't fling me in dat brier-patch."

They throw him into the briar patch, and Brer Rabbit is gone—free, happy, laughing at them once again.

My telling was based on the Disney versions of these characters that I had seen in the movie *Song of the South* when it was rereleased in the early 1970s (its premiere was in 1946). My more immediate source was a Little Golden Book that we had at home, called *Walt Disney's Uncle Remus* (Walt Disney Presents, 1974). When I told the story, I gave each of the narrator and three main characters a different voice and embodiment. My Brer Rabbit talked in a high, smart-talking voice. I was especially proud of and effective with Brer Bear—I stood with shoulders hunched, a blank look on my face, lips flapping, stammering.

In exploring the appeal of my performance of "De Tar Baby" to the rural community of my birth, I point to two important aspects that will not be developed in any detail. First, I performed with some skill—when I told my dad that I was writing about my storytelling in high school, and started to share with him some of my ideas for this chapter, he interrupted me and said, "Well, don't forget you were good." Second, the Brer Rabbit stories themselves are good. In his critical analysis of Uncle Remus as a Sambo figure, Boskin reminds his readers that

> Taken out of historical context, the Br'er Rabbit and related stories are engrossing, contain amusing and exciting situations, and strongly project many homiletic virtues. Connected to the trickster motif in African folklore … they further had the power of tradition and familiarity. … There is wisdom and strength, and considerable dignity as well, in the stories.
>
> *(1986, p. 103)*

This was a good story and I told it well. My audience was rural working people—it is not hard to imagine that they would enjoy a story about outsmarting the powerful.

The rural setting of both the Tar Baby story and my telling is also important. In looking at surviving minstrel lyrics and jokes from the antebellum period, historian David Roediger (1991) found that they were actually, surprisingly, quite tame and "certainly did not rival the sexuality and erotic punning in the works of contemporary literature by Melville or in the pulp fiction of the immensely popular George Lippard" (p. 121). For Roediger, the working-class audiences of the minstrel stage were less interested in some narrow form of sexual fulfillment than in a "range of broadly erotic pleasures—such as laughter, unfettered movement and contact with nature" (p. 122). Spectators of early minstrel shows were often recent immigrants to cities from rural areas in the United States or other countries. They were close enough to a 'preindustrial past' that they longed to see it, and its pleasures, represented on stage—especially since these pleasures, in their everyday lives in cities and industrial labor, were now lost to them.

My audience still lived in a rural setting, but that setting was changing. By the time I was a senior in high school, relatively few of my classmates were becoming farmers. The use of the land around Boonendam was shifting, with fewer and fewer farmers creating bigger and bigger farms. A growing number of people living in Boonendam commuted to work in a larger nearby city. My father thought that people his age liked hearing Brer Rabbit stories, in part, exactly because these stories evoked a relationship to the earth and nature that he thought was being lost. When he was young, by the time you were 10 or 11, when you weren't working, you spent summer days walking through woods, fooling around with your friends, maybe hunting rabbits.

Take what I have said so far seriously—I want it to stay with us even as I bring into focus how racialized this all was. Or maybe I am just stalling for now I, we, as white people, must come to grips with our own ugly creation.

⋆   ⋆   ⋆

Roediger (1991) argues that in the United States, in the period from colonial days through the Civil War, "working class formation and the development of a sense of whiteness went hand in hand" (p. 8). He interprets whiteness as bound up with, created in, the response of white workers to, first, a fear of dependency on wage labor and, second, the demands of a new capitalist work discipline.

The American Revolution made independence a powerful ideal, but white workers feared that the political independence promised by the Revolution would not be joined to an economic independence for them. What Roediger sees happening, then, is the attempt by workers not only to struggle with and define themselves in relation to society's white elites, but also, crucially, to define themselves in relation to, *define themselves against*, other workers who confronted even worse conditions than them—enslaved Africans. As Roediger puts it:

> Status and privileges conferred by race could be used to make up for alienating and exploitative class relationships, North and South. White workers could, and did, define and accept their class position by fashioning identities as "not slaves" and as "not Blacks."
>
> *(1991, p. 13)*

In other words, white workers would continue to confront alienating work. But they weren't slaves. And they weren't black; they were white. And they were compensated, as Whites, with what W.E.B. Du Bois describes as

> A sort of public and psychological wage. They were given public deference and titles of courtesy because they were white. They were admitted freely with all classes of white people to public functions, public parks, and the best schools. The police were drawn from their ranks. ... Their vote selected public officials, and while this had small effect upon the economic situation, it had great effect upon their personal treatment and the deference shown them.
>
> *(1935/1992, pp. 700–701)*

At the same time that white workers were creating a white identity by contrasting themselves to a black 'other,' they were also confronting a new capitalist system with escalating demands that workers embody an appropriate work ethic. Again, Blacks proved useful to white workers as they dealt with their own anxieties and ambivalence in relation to this new disciplinary regime.

White workers were responding to demands to give up ways of being, ways of living, that they were used to and enjoyed. Work—before *factory* work—might have included beer with lunch, might have been lightened and interrupted by jokes and storytelling, might have been called off altogether to get ready for a wedding party later that evening. Such behavior, as the Reverend Thandeka notes in her exploration of what white workers *lost* as their work moved into factories, was

> Typical of first-generation factory workers, native- or foreign-born. That work must be routinized, performed without regard to one's mood, and kept discrete from one's personal interests, separated from one's family life and values, was alien to preindustrial agrarian and peasant folk. … workers were constantly disciplined and reprimanded for their lazy, idle, nonproductive, and mindless ways.
>
> *(2001, pp. 63–64)*

If they wished to adhere to new definitions of what it meant to be a good worker, then white workers' desires, their pleasures, could not be a part of themselves anymore. Roediger (1991) traces how white workers projected onto Blacks— how they imagined Blacks as embodying—the ways of life and the pleasures and desires that white workers were reluctantly abandoning. For Roediger, then, the white working class responds to fears of dependency and to a capitalist work discipline by constructing "an image of the Black population as 'other'—as embodying the preindustrial, erotic, careless style of life the white worker hated and longed for" (p. 14).

This image, this 'other' born in the white imagination, in white dreams and nightmares, was the one who sang and danced and told stories on the minstrel stage. The one who haunted American literature.

He haunted Twain's *Huck Finn*. Ralph Ellison admired Twain for understanding and dramatizing powerfully, through Huck and his relationship to Jim, the conflict of property rights and person rights, slavery and democratic ethics, upon which the United States was founded. And he recognized that Twain portrayed Jim with considerable complexity and dignity. But Ellison argued that Jim was still that 'other,' that stereotype, created by Whites. Listen:

> It is not at all odd that this black-faced figure of white fun is for Negroes a symbol of everything they rejected in the white man's thinking about race. … Writing at a time when the blackfaced minstrel was still popular … Twain fitted Jim into the outlines of the minstrel tradition, and it is from behind this stereotype mask that we see Jim's dignity and human capacity—and Twain's complexity—emerge. Yet it is his source in this same tradition which creates that ambivalence between his identification as an adult and parent and his "boyish" naïveté, and which by contrast

makes Huck, with his street-sparrow sophistication, seem more adult. Certainly it upsets a Negro reader.

(1953/1995, p. 50)

A similar stance is taken by Joseph Boskin in relation to Joel Chandler Harris and the black-faced figure—Uncle Remus—that Harris fabricated to tell tales first told to him by black people living on a Georgia plantation. Boskin takes Harris at his word that he had no interest in portraying Blacks as "humorous foils." And, as Boskin (1986) notes: "The stature of the black storyteller [Uncle Remus] is impressive, his imagination powerful and uplifting, his tone self-assured. Harris's monologist contrasts with the gross exaggeration of the black male that appeared in many stories of the period" (pp. 103–104).

But in the end, Boskin argues, Harris's Uncle Remus only strengthened the stereotype—in this case, through the portrayal of a gentle black man who, as Harris (1911) himself puts it in his introduction to the Brer Rabbit tales, had "nothing but pleasant memories of the discipline of slavery" (p. xvii).

Boskin (1986) notes that Uncle Remus appears in the last decades of the nineteenth century, when "segregation was being riveted into the social fabric by legal, extra legal, and violent means" (p. 104). Jim Crow. Lynching. He reads Harris's Uncle Remus, this stereotype, as a sort of white wish, a white nostalgia, for the good old days when Blacks stayed on plantations.

Walt Disney optioned the rights to Harris's stories in 1939, and seven years later his own retelling of the Uncle Remus tales premiered in a segregated movie theater in Atlanta, Georgia. *Song of the South* combined animation and live action, with James Baskett in the lead role of Uncle Remus (and also performing the voice of the animated Brer Fox). Disney's film was supposed to take place in the same late 1800s as Harris's print version of Uncle Remus, but many who saw it assumed it took place during slavery. Indeed, even the studio seemed a bit confused—in one of its press releases, they described Uncle Remus as a slave. Whatever the confusion, Walt Disney declared the film a "monument to the Negro race."[5]

Many disagreed with Disney's declaration from the beginning. Clarence Muse, a black writer and principal screenwriter for the film, resigned when his attempts to mitigate stereotypical representations of black people in the film were rebuffed. Pickets accompanied premiers in other cities. A statement by the NAACP noted that the movie helped to "perpetuate a dangerously glorified picture of slavery"; Bosley Crowther of the *New York Times* believed that Disney's Uncle Remus was "just the sweetest and most wistful darky slave that ever stepped out of a sublimely unreconstructed fancy of the Old South" (cited in Brasch, 2000, pp. 279–280). But never mind.

The music score for the film was nominated for an Academy Award, and a song from the film—"Zip-a-Dee-Doo-Dah," which is drawn from the chorus of an 1834 minstrelsy song, "Zip Coon" (see Emerson, 1997)—won an Oscar for

Best Song. (I remember walking out of the theater into the bright sunlight and singing this song with my brother and sister as we walked to the car.) After the film's premier in 1946—and despite heavy and continual criticism—*Song of the South* was rereleased in 1956, 1972 (this must have been when I saw it), 1980, and 1986.

Song of the South spin-offs proliferated throughout American culture. There were record albums, children's books, a syndicated comic strip, and Disney depictions of Uncle Remus, Brer Fox, Brer Bear, and Brer Rabbit on stamps, beanbags, children's lunchboxes, porcelain, and pewter sculptures. There was an amusement park, Splash Mountain, with a fiberglass Briar Patch and a fast-food counter called "Brer Bar." There were five educational filmstrips, a sing-along videotape, and a one-hour made-for-TV docudrama of Harris's life, narrated by Walt Disney himself.[6]

Ellison believed that white people desperately needed the black-faced stereotype, *needed* Uncle Remus and Jim and Sambo and every other iteration found, as Boskin (1986) puts it, in "every nook and cranny of popular culture" (p. 11). For Ellison, white people needed them all in order to go on living as white Americans. They needed them continuously. Why? Ellison (1953/1995) thought that these stereotypes were much more than "simple racial clichés introduced into society by a ruling class to control political and economic realities" (p. 28). He thought that these clichés were certainly manipulated to that end, but that their significance went deeper, into the very ways that we make ourselves up as human beings with others. Ellison thought these counterfeit images of the black American were "projected aspects of an internal symbolic process through which, like a primitive tribesman dancing himself into the group frenzy necessary for battle, the white American prepares himself emotionally to perform a social role" (pp. 27–28).

I am standing on the stage in front of my community. I am Uncle Remus. I am playing at the stereotype. But this is also serious. I am preparing my audience for battle. I am preparing them, emotionally, so they, too, can perform—perform their social role of being white. What is so punishing about this role that we need to screw our emotions to the sticking place to take it up? The group frenzy of the primitive tribesman helps him forget, forget his fear, his self, so he can do battle. What do we need to forget? Ellison continues:

> Color prejudice springs not from the stereotype alone, but from an internal psychological state; not from misinformation alone, but from an inner need to believe. … Hence, whatever else the Negro stereotype might be as a social instrumentality, it is also a key figure in a magic rite by which the white American seeks to resolve the dilemma arising between his democratic beliefs and certain antidemocratic practices, between his acceptance of the sacred democratic belief that all men are created equal and his treatment of every tenth man as though he were

not. [...] Perhaps the object of the stereotype is not so much to crush the Negro as to console the white man.

(1953/1995, pp. 28, 41)

In other words, as white people, we need stereotypes of people of color to give us relief from the strain of participating in and benefiting from a society that at every moment disregards a founding principle—that all people are created equal. Racial stereotypes enable us to continue believing in democracy even as we betray it. At the core of white racial identities, then, is a dilemma, a conflict, an ambivalence—a belief in and desire for equality in America, poised against the evidence, all around us, of massive inequality.

As the black-faced minstrel (even without blacking up), I could evoke carefree, lazy days, could conjure escape from the drudgery of farm work, factory time, and respectability. But I was only playing in black, so I simultaneously assured and reassured my audience that we—though we and those white folk who came before us worked in fields and factories and had little money, little power—we were free, white; not slaves, black. I was playing at blackness, ultimately mocking it, the magician with hands that—poof—disappeared our guilt.

I believe this to be true. And yet I cannot let this stand as a final word, an *only-that* word.

★   ★   ★

I was a good storyteller and the Tar Baby story was a good one—it reminded us of the pleasures of an intimate relation with the land, and it celebrated frustrating the appetites of the powerful, celebrated laughing even as their gaping jaws closed fast on our tail.

I could have done other things in these speech contests. I could have given an extemporaneous speech, developed a serious monologue, read poetry or prose. Mr. Archer is one of the important teachers in my life, and when I was a senior in high school, he wanted me to do something more serious than storytelling. He wanted me to work with him and a few other students in another category of the speech contests—playacting. It was a serious category, with serious material.

I had taken World and American Literature classes with Mr. Archer. I had worked closely with him on sophisticated and elaborate stagings of musicals throughout my four years of high school. My senior year, with Mr. Archer directing, I played Professor Henry Higgins in a production of *My Fair Lady*—a musical very much about how high and low ways of talking and acting expose and determine your place in life. No character in the play was more committed to explicating and enforcing this division than my character, Higgins.

When it came time to begin work on the speech contests, I said no to Mr. Archer. He was disappointed (to me, at the time, it seemed almost that he was disgusted) with my decision to tell stories instead.

And this story—the one I am trying to tell you right now—keeps spinning outward, becomes, it seems, almost impossible to tell without telling you everything about how we all made up our lives in Boonendam High School, in Boonendam, Wisconsin, in 1979. It *does* become impossible to tell, because everything is connected. A limited, partial rendering, then.

I was a top student, the quarterback in football, starting point guard on the basketball team. I played leads in musicals and went to state not just in speech contests but also music competitions. And yet I never felt like I belonged. I could not have expressed it this way then, but now I know that I was already engaged in the struggle that has defined my life in school, all the way from elementary through graduate school, and on into my life as a professor. I was struggling with the offer, made by school, to join the middle class. I was struggling with its demand that I remake (or at least hide) my working-class insides.

When I decided to tell a Brer Rabbit story—at that moment, in that space—I rejected that demand. (Please—I understand how small this seems—understand that I was still performing the successful student as I took up another extracurricular activity.) This rejection took the form of choosing both a low-class event (storytelling) over a high-class one (drama) and a low-class story (a black folk tale) instead of all the other stories I could have told (and that I heard everyone else telling, from Boonendam to Madison).

Again, my decision, my action, was mostly impulsive, unconscious.[7] At the time, I only knew that storytelling felt better, felt closer to me, that it connected me to places and people I cared about. And I knew that something pleasurable, something important even, was going on in the Brer Rabbit stories and that this pleasure and significance had something to do with resisting authority.

The impulses and desires that led me to Brer Rabbit stories resemble, echo, I think, those of early white blackface performers. I say *early* blackface performers because historians W.T. Lhamon (1998, 2003) and Dale Cockrell (1997) argue forcefully that early blackface minstrelsy (before the mid 1840s) was quite different than later minstrelsy. Lhamon (2003), for example, has uncovered and collected early minstrel plays that Lott and others did not have access to—and these plays display not a hatred for black people, but a rather consistent solidarity with them. Lhamon argues that the plays represent the "earliest American written portraits of blacks by whites that center blacks positively" and that, in them,

> Blackened actors grab center stage, hold it, and defend it. They speak more cunningly than their stilted white counterparts. They achieve their own ends—distinct from white ends—and win audience approval for taking care of business. They are active within the unbalanced power and social strain of their era—tensions both lampooned and seriously addressed in the plays and songs. And against all odds they win their contests.
>
> *(2003, pp. viii–ix)*

Traditional images of the sites, participants, and audiences of minstrel acts are also being revised in this scholarship. U.S. presidents, including Lincoln, had been entertained by minstrel troupes, but those performances were a great distance—a great social distance—from early blackface minstrelsy. For the earliest shows were in the roughest bars and taverns, enacted on small stages in the corner that raised performers a foot or two above the crowd. That crowd was mixed, racially. And the performers? Lhamon writes that

> Contrary to the disinformation that blacks were excluded from American stages, in fact, black and "yellow" performers, along with those whites in blackface, were on view every night in the Five Points dives [in lower Manhattan], just as they all mingled in these low audiences. The generalization about the exclusion of blacks from American theatre is another instance of historical attention limited to polite reality.
>
> *(1998, p. 158)*

The history of theater and culture may ignore what was going on in venues deemed not-polite, but at the time, journalists and politicians were keenly interested in these impolite pursuits. Why? They sensed danger, rebellion even. They worried, as white elites had since at least the beginnings of slavery, about cross-racial solidarity—that young, poor Whites might align themselves with free and enslaved Blacks rather than with their white superiors. What has come down to us as an important means of keeping black people in their place—blackface minstrelsy as expropriation of black culture for the enrichment of white performers, blackface minstrelsy as disseminator of the black stereotype—began as something quite different, or at least as something much more complex.

White performers put on the black mask, in the beginning, not so much to mock or degrade black people and black cultural practices, but because they were attracted to them and their ways of moving in the world. These white working youth saw in black ways of being clues as to how they themselves might respond to a world not set up for them either. From behind the mask, they mocked their white bosses and abused society's white leaders. As Cockrell (1997) puts it: "New research makes clear the resistance of the urban working class in Jacksonian America to industrialization, with its clocks, bosses, subordination, grimness, and 'wage slavery' (their term, not mine). Minstrelsy attacked these institutions" (p. 169).

One of the first and most famous blackface performers, T.D. 'Daddy' Rice, took the stage as a character named 'Jim Crow,' and when Lhamon (1998) traced this name back through time, he found that before Jim Crow was used to name our system of apartheid in the South, he was a black trickster figure. To 'jump Jim Crow' was to invoke this trickster, this upsetter of the system. Thus, at the beginning, when Whites blacked up and jumped Jim Crow, they were not engaged in a project of putting black people in their place—they were engaged in a project of disruption, and displaying cross-racial solidarity in the process. For Lhamon, these performers were

> Not so much racist as something like its opposite, or something besides. Well before abolitionism in the United States had gathered steam … these white working youths in the west Atlantic were choosing to join with perceived blackness. … The reasons and functions of this choice were not simple. But it was this choosing among themselves to delineate their cross-racial mutuality … that angered the magazine writers and prominent politicians. … Minstrelsy certainly accompanied cruel domination, but it did not start that way. Rather, it began in order to work out, and express, mixed feelings of identification and fascination.
>
> *(1998, p. 187–188)*

The title of Lani Guinier and Gerald Torres's (2002) book *The Miner's Canary: Enlisting Race, Resisting Power, Transforming Democracy* references the practice of miners taking canaries with them into mines. The canaries could warn the miners of danger because their bodies responded more quickly to poisons in the environment than the miners' bodies would. Guinier and Torres argue that oppressed people in the United States take up a similar position to canaries in mines, and that white society must start attending to what these people know about our toxic society because, eventually, these poisons will kill us all. They imagine a new movement, led by people of color and joined by white people smart enough to pay attention.

I find Guinier and Torres's imagery and arguments persuasive and powerful. But looked at historically, and especially with reference to poor and working white people, you would have to add that white people have always been paying attention to black people and have always been attracted to them.[8] This is the 'love' half of Lott's (1995) *Love and Theft*. For Lhamon (2003), early blackface minstrelsy displays how "politically disfranchised and economically excluded Americans have long felt attraction for black ways of moving through trouble" (p. x).

Blackface minstrelsy began this way, but the cross-racial solidarity didn't hold. The process of 'othering' black people, as described earlier with the help of Roediger (1991), ground on. White journalists and politicians tried to account for the alarming popularity of early minstrelsy by spinning it as simply good old racist fun—and they largely succeeded. There was clearly money to be made, and eventually blackface minstrelsy moved to 'proper' theaters, attracted 'proper' audiences (including well-to-do Whites), and propagated 'proper' messages about the relations of Blacks and Whites (that is, divided, not mixed).[9] After hopeful and expansive beginnings, blackface minstrelsy went the way of, propped up, the larger white supremacist society.

We cannot and should not deny the viciousness of blackface minstrelsy, especially the forms it took *after* it moved from raised platforms in low-class taverns to the stages of more respectable theaters. At the same time, we, as white people, are probably doomed to repeat ourselves if we do not understand both the wrong turns we made and the paths we abandoned too soon. Lhamon, with reference to Ellison's famous essay "Change the Joke and Slip the Yoke" (in Ellison, 1953/1995), puts it this way: "There is no way to slip the blackface yoke when the acknowledged history of the process lacks its hopeful early moves" (Lhamon, 2003, p. x).

But again—there is danger in even these hopeful early moves; there is always the possibility that they will lead to what critical educator and race theorist bell hooks (1992) calls "eating the Other," where the cultures and bodies of oppressed groups become commodified and consumed by those with more status and privilege. This possibility, this danger, presses down on the historical scholarship on early blackface minstrelsy and forces slightly different interpretations of it—a difference I earlier ignored. Cockrell (1997), inspired by Mikhail Bakhtin's (1984) work on how the folk subvert and resist the official ideas and values of those in power, tends to interpret early minstrelsy as *cross-racial solidarity*—in the sense that it is of a piece with all the other ways that black and white poor people often stood (and lived and drank and fought and lay in bed) together in large cities, and against white superiors who sought to use them and make their lives miserable. In contrast, Lhamon (1998) writes about mutuality, identification, and fascination and is more interested that early blackface minstrelsy not be *reduced to only racism*— "not so much racist as something like its opposite, or something besides" (p. 187). He is less interested in claiming some strong alignment of white working youth with people of color.

It is possible to be attracted to another group's ways of being and moving in the world without taking up their fate with your own. Lott (1995) reminds us that when all is said and done, "cultural expropriation is the minstrel show's central fact, and we should not lose sight of it" (p. 19). In the real world, Brer Rabbit lives a nightmare and gets eaten, over and over, by Brer Fox and Brer Bear.[10]

The point (and the problem), then, is how the obvious attraction white people have for black people and black cultural forms might lead to reliable cross-racial alliances rather than to a hardening of racial division and stereotypes. A small step is recognizing that white people's relations to people of color and their cultures are seldom simple and are usually characterized by attraction, envy, and desire as well as fear and rejection. The portrait of racial identity that emerges from the research on blackface minstrelsy allows us to recognize and theorize the profound *ambivalence* that has characterized white thinking and feeling about black people in the United States.

★　　★　　★

My path has not been straight. I have had to interpret, retell, the story of my storytelling three times, and even this seems only preliminary to making better sense of becoming white with black materials. My first telling traced a rural sensibility that I shared with my audience, and that we shared with the immigrants to cities in the early 1800s who made up much of blackface minstrelsy's original audiences. Then, a sharp turn to how white working people responded to a fear of dependency on wage labor and to the demands of a new capitalist work discipline by investing a black stereotype with everything they hated and longed for. Ellison said that we, as white Americans, need this stereotype, all the time, to give us some relief from the guilt of participating in and benefiting from a society that at every moment betrays a founding principle—that all people are created equal. Finally, another turn to the impulses and desires of early blackface minstrelsy, where white working youth tried on black ways of moving in the world in order to thumb their noses at disapproving, disdainful white superiors and, with a sideways glance, to signal cross-racial solidarity with their black mentors.

I want to try again. I want to be a different sort of storyteller than a white-faced/black-faced Uncle Remus. With Delores and Frank in the next chapter, and then with the rest, I will tell stories of learning to be, and being, white—stories of fear and scapegoating, of desire and longing. I will draw again on Ralph Ellison, as well as the Reverend Thandeka and others, in order to make sense of these strange, conflicted things we've become as white people—and everywhere around us, past and present, this horrific violence we do to others and to ourselves.

★   ★   ★

I am on the stage.

I am Uncle Remus.

Blacks from Georgia plantations may have been whispering softly to me and my audience, but much louder, much more insistent, were the white folk, North and South, past and present, who, like those sitting in front of me, worked too hard, too long, for little gain save some pride in their survival. And unfortunately, they, we, instead of standing with, identifying with others who have endured generations of horrors and worked too hard, too long, in a country that cared little whether they lived or died as long as someone did the work—instead of standing with them, we took pride and comfort in not being them, in not being black.

We make love. We murder. We forget, or try to, so we can go on being white.

Notes

1 My parents would sometimes laugh and tease me when I was a child by saying that they named me after a weed. Timothy is a coarse, common grass, native to Europe, that came to North America with early English colonists. It was (and still is) used as cattle feed and as hay for horses. Timothy, the plant, is naturalized throughout most of the United States and southern Canada—with *naturalized*, in this case, meaning that it now grows wild where it was not indigenous. Thus, the name and teasing my parents bestowed upon me could not have been more apt—I am coarse and descended from common white folk who now grow wild on a continent to which we were not indigenous. Call me Timothy. Yes, my intent is to evoke the first words—"Call me Ishmael"—of Herman Melville's (1851/1949) novel *Moby Dick*, as well as gesture toward that novel's complex treatment of whiteness and capitalism (see, for example, Morrison, 1989). And yes, the title of my book and the last sentence of my forethought echo W.E.B. Du Bois's (1903/1997) *The Souls of Black Folk* and the last sentence of his forethought.

2 Even closer, geographically, is Mankato, Minnesota, site of the largest mass execution in U.S. history. On the day after Christmas in 1862, 38 Dakota men were hanged for their attempts to defend their Dakota homeland as part of the U.S.–Dakota War (see Waziyatawin, 2008). This chapter conceptualizes white racial identity along a black–white axis—see Deloria (1988) and Frost (2005) for explorations of white Americans' identities in relation to appropriations and distortions of American Indian cultures.

3 The claim here is not, of course, for any particular resemblance to black speech and movement. Instead, I was performing the black stereotype. In its review of the Disney movie *Song of the South*, upon which my storytelling was based, *Ebony* pointed to the Uncle Remus character as an "Uncle Tom-Aunt Jemima caricature, complete with … a profusion of 'dis' and 'dat' talk" (cited in Brasch, 2000, p. 280).

4 I made up this introduction. The book I used to memorize the story, *Walt Disney's Uncle Remus* (Walt Disney Presents, 1974), begins: "Way down deep in de brier-patch is de home of Brer Rabbit. He is a smart feller, but he get on de nerves of Brer Bear and Brer Fox" (n.p.). Later quotes from the story are taken from this book.

5 See Brasch (2000, pp. 274–287) for a fascinating account of the making of and response to *Song of the South* (the Disney quote appears on p. 278). I draw heavily on Brasch here.

6 The one accommodation the Disney studio seems to have made to all the criticism is that it has never released the film on videotape in the United States—it did, however, do so in 1996 in Europe and Japan (see Brasch, 2000, p. 285). For one of many defenses of the film on the internet, see www.songofthesouth.net/movie/overview/defense.html.

7 John Dewey (1916/1966, p. 77) reminds us that

> Activity begins in an impulsive form. … It does not know what it is about; that is to say, what are its interactions with other activities. An activity which brings education or instruction with it makes one aware of some of the connections which had been imperceptible.

8 I grant that they may have been and may still be paying the wrong sort of attention—that is, watching how to resist and to survive with style, rather than listening to critiques of the system.

9 I am simplifying here. Lhamon (1998) argues that the oppositional and mixing aspects of minstrelsy were never lost, but just forced to be much more subtle. And Lott (1995) reminds us that you cannot play at being black without coming into contact with blackness—so mixing is always there, even in mockery.

10 In his brilliant essay "Uncle Remus and the Malevolent Rabbit," Bernard Wolfe (1949) argues that in the figure of Uncle Remus, Harris displays the desperate wish by white Americans to be loved by the same people who they continually seek to destroy. So Harris puts a loving smile on Uncle Remus, but the smile only partially hides the mortal struggle that is being engaged between black and white America in the figures of Brer Rabbit and Brer Fox. Harris listened well enough to black storytellers that Brer Rabbit's malevolence comes through in the tales—he scalds, burns, tortures his enemies. Walt Disney had to tone all this down, sanitize and emasculate the angry Rabbit.

2

WE LEARNED THE WRONG THINGS AND WENT UNDERGROUND

I talked with Delores in the small library of her school. For my interviews with Frank, we met in an unused office. Both were educators, but Delores sat still and composed as we talked, with a dry sense of humor that it took me a while to recognize (then I laughed quite a bit); while Frank gestured with his arms and hands and made faces—he told me early on that, no matter what else we discussed, he had a story he needed to tell before our interviews together were over (I will share this story in Chapter 4).

In what follows, I begin with Delores's stories of being a student at a small state teachers college in Wisconsin. Delores attended State College in the late 1960s, and her undergraduate years included first-hand experiences with race riots and civil rights and antiwar protests. Delores had been afraid to participate in protests and tried to be what she called an "innocent bystander." This stance was challenged later by her daughter (when her daughter was in college) and by Delores herself, especially as she considered her moral responsibilities as a religious person and educator.

I call upon Delores's stories to explore white people's fear of people of color. White fear has usually been understood in terms of white people's response to a threatening, stereotyped racial 'other'—in other words, white people create a scary stereotype that then is feared by white people. I argue that, in addition, white fear results from acts of violence by white authority against its own white community. Drawing on the Reverend Thandeka's (2001) account of how white children and youth learn to be white, I analyze how white desire for love and solidarity with people of color is policed and suppressed, resulting in fear and a divided, ambivalent white self.

Fear, a fragmented and conflicted self—not exactly happy results of a civil rights struggle meant to secure, finally, in real life, America's sacred principle that all people are created equal. Sociologist Eduardo Bonilla-Silva (2001, 2003) is similarly skeptical about what white people learned from the civil rights era. He has challenged the results of large-scale surveys that indicate that white people's attitudes toward people of color have changed for the better since the 1960s. He argues, instead, that a deep, recalcitrant and racist ideology still characterizes white people's thinking and feeling. What *has* changed, according to Bonilla-Silva (2003), is how white people talk about race. Whatever they actually think and feel, white people have taken on a new style of talk, a "language of color-blindness" which "avoids racist terminology" and tries to sound non-racist through "semantic moves such as 'I am not racist, but,' 'Some of my best friends are …,' 'I am not black, but,' 'Yes and no,' or 'Anything but race'" (p. 70).

Unfortunately, Frank's stories, about how white people live and move in the world four decades after Delores was in college, tend to confirm Bonilla-Silva's work—especially Bonilla-Silva's sense of a polite, non-racist surface hiding an impolite, racist depth.[1] Much of Frank's talk about white people and white selves was organized in terms of *up* and *down*. For Frank, white people talked and moved in two primary realms or spaces: a high space in which Frank thought you needed to be "politically correct" and a low space in which, as Frank put it, things took on "a whole different tone." Stereotypes. Racist humor.

In the previous chapter, I argued, with Ralph Ellison's (1953/1995) help, that stereotypes of people of color enabled white people to continue to feel good about America because these stereotypes mediated the tension, the gap, between democratic beliefs and antidemocratic practices. Ellison also believed that stereotypes helped white people feel good about themselves. He thought of racist humor and the use of stereotypes as scapegoating rituals—small rites white people performed in order to raise themselves up by putting racial others down. However, these scapegoating rituals never quite worked completely or once and for all to reassure of white superiority. Hence, the continual needy repetition. In Frank's low space, then, the sound of laughter and scapegoating and desperation, that "whole different tone."

★   ★   ★

People from Boonendam often thought of big cities as dangerous, as places to be feared. William talked about this fear of big cities the most directly, and I take up, in the next chapter, how he feared big cities because he imagined himself as necessarily, inevitably, in a fight for scarce resources with the black men who lived there—black men who, like him, had little wealth.

Toward the end of her preparation to become a teacher, Delores lived for a semester in what she considered a big city, and her sense of danger might certainly have been heightened by the fact that there were race riots and curfews imposed there as she reported for student teaching. However, and in contrast to William, *fear* and *race* did not seem joined for Delores because of imagined or real conflict with people of color. Fear was important to her experience as a white person in other ways.

When she was at college, with student protests a regular part of life in Wisconsin universities, her parents told her that "if you're in trouble, you do not come home."

DELORES: So I was there in the last half of the '60s, and you heard about race riots and there was the whole Oktoberfest downtown ... and knowing my parents very well is, if you're in trouble, you do not come home. If you got yourself in trouble there was no one phone—we didn't have a phone.

TIMOTHY: Right.

DELORES: So there was no phone call home. The teacher support I had from the high school was the same way, you know, "this is what you do, we'll help you do this," and I could call with academic questions and writing papers, but—

TIMOTHY: You took care of yourself.

DELORES: Yeah, yeah. ... It was made very clear to me by my parents that "if we ever see you on TV or you get picked up, you're not coming home." There's no phone call home.

The danger for Delores, what was feared here, was losing the support and help of her parents and former teachers. Delores's sense of vulnerability was only heightened by the fact that she was not sure if she could count on the support of her family and community in the first place. Delores told me that, at the time, very few young women from Boonendam and farming families like hers went to college; that her parents were confused by her desire to get a college education; and that some in the community imagined the purpose of college for women in patriarchal terms, as exemplified by the parish priest who asked Delores when she returned home for Christmas break during her first year if she had found a husband yet.

In the above, Delores suggested that her parents would make no distinction between, on the one hand, getting "in trouble" during Oktoberfest (where *trouble*, I assume, meant getting drunk and doing something stupid) and, on the other hand, getting "in trouble" for participating in the struggle for civil rights. We do not know what Delores's parents would actually have done, but the scene Delores imagined—what she feared—was that her transgression, whether political or involving alcohol, might even show up on the evening news and that her parents' response would be to abandon her to whatever trouble she had gotten herself into—"you're not coming home."

Delores also admitted to being quite afraid of the police, who she perceived as being willing to inflict violence not just on protestors but also on unfortunate onlookers. Years later, when Delores's daughter also went to State College and took a class that examined the local movements and protests that her mother had lived through, Delores's decision to not participate, actively, bothered her daughter.

Delores told the story to me as a humorous one, as a sort of joke on herself, but it seemed to me that there was embarrassment for her in the story as well:

> In the center of the dorm complex on that street corner—what started out was food riots in the cafeteria. And we had heard about it as you do and you know, "not going to go over there," and I tried to—my daughter just laughs at this you know. You don't understand that at that time civil rights were not recognized the way they are—if you were just standing there watching, but they could just pick you up and take you in, that was enough. I said "watch the '68 Democratic Convention tapes"—and she is in social studies so she knew what I was talking about, but she still laughed at this.

Delores described a time of student unrest at State College. College administration attempted to enforce a uniform student conduct code amidst food riots and increasing opposition to the Vietnam War and the draft. Delores asserted that "civil rights," even for white people like herself, "were not recognized" and that "if you were just standing there watching," the police could "pick you up and take you in."

I want to make as clear as possible what Delores wanted her daughter, who was studying to be a social studies teacher at State College, to learn by watching videotapes of what had happened at the 1968 Democratic Convention in Chicago.[2] I asked her about this later in our first interview and again in our second. Delores used the phrase "innocent bystander," and we will see later how this phrase became a source of trouble for Delores.

DELORES: Was that the [Rodney] King case in California where a man was stopped for a traffic violation and the police beat him? And you know, not wanting, no, I don't want to go to the Democratic Convention in 1968. And then showing my daughter those film clips and saying—"now what part of that do you want to be involved in?" Many innocent people being beaten and killed during the Martin Luther King era, and I would have considered myself an innocent bystander and [exhales deeply] the Vietnam War protests—

TIMOTHY: I'm trying to figure out the, you know, you mentioned Martin Luther King's time and then the Vietnam War protests—the, the innocent bystanders that are hurt—who was hurting them? I mean, when you think of it that way, who's, who's hurting them?

DELORES: Well certainly the images of the police with their sticks and their dogs—when you think of Rosa Parks, when you think of—what was the name of the little black girl going to that school—Ruby Bridges—when you think of Ruby Bridges and those adults—

TIMOTHY: White adults.

DELORES: Those adults that antagonized her all the way to school and then you needed the federal marshals there to protect her.

TIMOTHY: Right.

DELORES: Now, to me, if you need to call out the federal marshals for protection, that's a serious situation. I mean, I had never heard of federal marshals before. So I would say certainly that child Ruby Bridges was far braver than I was.

The events and images Delores linked together here are striking. They form a sort of defense against her daughter's laughter at and questioning of Delores for wanting to remain an "innocent bystander." Delores connected the vicious beating of Rodney King by Los Angeles police officers in 1991 to the 1968 Democratic Convention in Chicago, and then she joined these to "images of the police with their sticks and their dogs" and the "innocent people being beaten and killed during the Martin Luther King era." Clearly, Delores meant for her daughter to consider the violence that police and others were willing to rain down not only on protestors, but anyone standing close at hand.

In this part of the interview, one of my questions clumped together, around the term "innocent," people who Delores actually seemed to think of as separate groups. One group that Delores considered innocent included people like Rosa Parks and Ruby Bridges,[3] who were innocent in the sense that they were actively trying to do good, not bad. The other innocent group included Delores herself, and this was made up of "innocent bystanders"—people not directly participating in protest. And these were in contrast to a third group that was not innocent, which included white police and other white adults who were violently opposing the protest and dissent of Rosa Parks, Ruby Bridges, the Reverend King, and others.

It was Delores's bystanding, her lack of active involvement' in protest, that bothered Delores's daughter.

DELORES: When she went to State College, she took a Vietnam course and it was three pieces of literature that these Vietnam, these three Vietnam vets had written—one was *The Things They Carried*—I've forgotten what the other book was, and then there was a book of poetry by one of them, and I remember she brought it home and I'd read that because—I'd think, okay, these were all authors around State College—Wisconsin authors.[4]

TIMOTHY: That's cool.

DELORES: Yeah, it was a very cool course. So the one on poetry, when they finished that one, they had to write a poem so she wrote about me not getting involved, and the title of the poem was "From the Other Side of the Street." And the professor was just very intrigued when—first the content of the poem and you know it wasn't long—"How did you come up with this idea?" and then she said it was really based on her mother who had been at State College in the late '60s. ... But I said my, my involvement with civil rights was really one of fear because you could—you didn't talk about freedom of speech and you didn't talk about being an innocent bystander ...

the riots were traveling around. Now there had been—was that before or after the bombing—when was Kent State?

TIMOTHY: I don't have a great sense of—

DELORES: Yeah—but see there was the bombing at the UW [University of Wisconsin, Madison]—you really didn't want to get involved in something like that. And of course Madison was the most predominant, sure—and it was almost as though, you know, if you're in a university and they're not doing anything, you know, what kind of university?—

TIMOTHY: [laughter]

DELORES: So State College, the food riots—that was, that's pretty tame, you know, but "no, not going over there, not getting involved in that." So like I said, my daughter who is in social studies just had a hoot over that—until I told her to look at the clips of the '68 Democratic Convention in Chicago. And I think my feelings on that was, you know, I was—at the time I couldn't say it like this—now I would say the dignity of every human being is within that person from birth on, you know, there is that dignity. At the time I couldn't say it like that, but I think I grew up with, that's what I believed in—and there was this amount of fear.

In the above, Delores referenced the Sterling Hall bombing at the University of Wisconsin, on August 24, 1970, by four young people in protest against the university's connections with the U.S. military. A physics professor was killed, with three others suffering injuries. She also referenced the shootings a few months earlier at Kent State University in Ohio. Members of the Ohio National Guard shot at students, four of whom were killed and another nine wounded. Some of the students involved had been protesting the American invasion of Cambodia; others were observing or walking nearby.

Note the tension, the ambivalence, Delores gets to right at the end of this part of the interview. A tension between believing in the inherent dignity of every human being and a fear of the violence that might be done to you if you struggle to change a world that doesn't honor this dignity.

Delores's experiences during college provided her with opportunities to participate in the various movements of the time. Her response was to try to be what she called an "innocent bystander." By this, she meant that she was often in agreement with people of color and others who were protesting, but that she did not participate, in support of them, in public actions.[5]

Her daughter had called this stance, this moral position of "innocent bystander," into question. And there was more trouble for Delores in the interviews with me when she realized that a professional development program in which she was participating—one aimed at reducing bullying among students— also had something to say about being an "innocent bystander."

The program challenged values that Delores and I had grown up with as children—values which included that you weren't supposed to tattle or 'tell' on other children. But the professional development program was promoting the idea of creating a "telling school" in which children were encouraged to talk with adults if they saw someone else being bullied. What Delores realized within our conversations was that, within the anti-bullying program, there was no such thing as an "innocent bystander" and that this had implications for her long-standing view of herself, especially in racial matters, as just such a bystander.

DELORES: The teacher meeting we went to on Thursday had to do with bullying. Oh has that taken a different approach ... how after all your life you worked with "don't tattle, it's not right to tattle, you shouldn't be tattling," and now you want to tell children that you are going to develop a telling school. And there is a difference between tattling and reporting, but how to reverse that culture? And that you know the number one prevention strategy against bullying is that there are no longer innocent bystanders—and I know that I've used that word and we've talked about that here—and now to try to enculturate that there is no innocent bystander, that you have a responsibility, if you are not reporting bullying then you are part of it. Now to turn that around—

TIMOTHY: That's really tough. I mean, that's a tough moral problem—

DELORES: It's staggering. I mean it just goes, it goes against things that I've told my children, that we've told our children, about tattling.

In our second interview, I asked Delores about her use of "innocent bystander" in relation to both her experiences with protests in the 1960s and the anti-bullying program.

DELORES: Yes, I was not an innocent bystander when I was watching that at State College. And, uh, I was there—there was something that made me be there, and whereas I saw myself as an innocent bystander—and yet I can remember telling my daughter that as far as the police were concerned, there were no innocent bystanders, that they could pull you in. There wasn't such a thing as your civil rights, you know, that if you were there, you were part of that.

TIMOTHY: Yeah, but it flips the other way too—that if we have to, we have to, if we bought into the way the bullying program thinks of it, there is also a set of moral obligations we'd take up. That we sort of couldn't be like an innocent bystander that chose, in some sense, to do nothing, right? That there's, that's a tough one, you know? When do we—

DELORES: When do we tell? When don't we tell? Well if it harms somebody else, you should tell—

TIMOTHY: Who do we tell?

DELORES: And there's the whole thing—what's going to happen to me if I tell? You know, what's going to happen to me if I protest?

At the end of this segment of the interview, Delores again raised the issue of fear and a concern for her own safety. Against the backdrop of historical examples of police violence against protest—and in other parts of her interviews, she also discussed recent examples of increased government surveillance and efforts to muffle and stifle dissent—against this backdrop, she asked, "What's going to happen to me if I protest?"

★   ★   ★

Sociologist Ruth Frankenberg (1993) asserts that white people's fear of people of color needs "careful analysis, both because of its prevalence and because it is an inversion of reality" (p. 60). In what follows, I summarize Frankenberg's understanding of white fear, which links fear to stereotypes of people of color. Then, I argue that Delores's fear is better accounted for with reference to Thandeka's (2001) work on white racial identity. I develop an analysis of white fear that highlights the violence and policing function of white authority in relation to its own white community.

Frankenberg (1993) considers white fear an "element of racist discourse"— specifically, racist discourse that is linked to "essentialist racism … the idea that people of color are fundamentally Other than white people: different, inferior, less civilized, less human, more animal, than whites" (p. 61). For Frankenberg, the imagery and stereotypes of essentialist racism are produced and renewed throughout U.S. history as a pretext for white hostility against people of color, and especially in relation to black men. She notes that

> A key aspect of white women's fear of Black men has to do with the persistent, racist image of the Black man as rapist. As Angela Davis has clarified, the production of this myth took place alongside the abolition of slavery and efforts by Black and white people toward reconstruction of the southern economy and polity along more racially egalitarian lines. The lynching of Black people was a means of social and political repression; accusations of rape were used as alibis for what were in effect politically motivated death squads. A discourse ostensibly about threat or danger was in fact a rationale for repression or control.
>
> *(1993, p. 61)*

For Frankenberg, white fear of people of color is an "inversion of reality" because, as she notes, "in general, people of color have far more to fear from white people than vice versa" (p. 60). And her analysis leads her to theorize white fear as one of the forms that race privilege and racism may take (along with other forms such as educational and economic inequality, maintenance of all-white neighborhoods, and verbal assertions of white supremacy). In other words, *white privilege and racism produce white fear*. A menacing, counterfeit image of the 'other' is created by the white community, which is then feared by members of that same community.

   I do not question any aspect of Frankenberg's account of white fear—the prevalence of this fear, how it is an inversion of reality, and how it emerges in response to stereotypes that were created by white people as part of efforts to repress and control people of color. However, Delores's stories and experiences suggest that Frankenberg's analysis of white fear needs to be supplemented, extended. I think that Thandeka's (2001) theorizing of how white people learn to be white is extremely helpful for this expanded understanding of white fear.

   What Thandeka (2001) heard, over and over, when she asked white people to recount early experiences with race were stories of unease and conflict and heartbreak. Often, the conflict and heartbreak were not loud, but quiet. And often, it was not clear at the time exactly what the problem was. For me, one of the most potent stories that Thandeka shared was from a man named Jack who had told her a story about his fifth birthday:

> When Jack was five, his parents gave him a birthday party and invited his relatives with their children. He remembers going to the gate of his backyard and calling his friends over to join them. His friends, black, entered the yard. Jack became aware of how uncomfortable his parents were with the presence of his friends among them. He knew he had somehow done something wrong and was sorry.
>
> *(2001, p. 5)*

This story is striking and significant for at least three reasons. First, it is easy to imagine this little child, Jack, running through his backyard, smiling, yelling to his friends to come to his party. And it is exactly at this moment of joy, this moment of calling out to and embracing his friends—it is exactly at this moment of expansiveness that he learned that he had somehow done something wrong. Second, the story is striking because of the child's uncertainty as to what he had done wrong. These were his friends. He played with them, and obviously, before this, he had not thought that his parents had a problem with these friendships. Jack ran to the gate to call his friends, but when they walked among his family—I imagine these three little boys walking in a line, weaving through all the white bodies dressed up to celebrate Jack's birthday—he realized that he had done something wrong. He did not know exactly what it was, but he knew that it had something to do with his friends, his black friends. Finally, Jack was sorry. Jack did not know what he had done wrong, but he was sorry. He did not want his parents to be uncomfortable. He wanted to be a good boy.

   Drawing both on psychoanalytic theory and historical work on whiteness and social class, Thandeka (2001) characterizes what happened to Jack as 'abuse' and argues that white selves are built out of the racial abuse by white adults of their own children and youth. That is, white children's desires do not, in the beginning, recognize the racial boundaries and hierarchies of our society. But soon enough, white children like Jack are confronted by adult disapproval that suggests that desires for friendship and love that point outside the white community are wrong and that if the child persists in pursuing such desires, then adult support and love may be withheld. Because this is often not dramatic and explicit, and because our society and schools provide few opportunities to explore how we think and feel about race, white children become white adults with a deep, unnamed confusion and shame about racial matters.

Thandeka traces the origins of white racial abuse against its own community back to the fears of white elites, at least since the beginning of slavery, that poor and working-class Whites might recognize common cause with people of color, in opposition to their white superiors. In response to these fears, white elites have engaged in a series of actions that divide and conquer common people, often by granting limited standing and privilege to white folk while denying it to their black sisters and brothers.

For example, laws in colonial Virginia gave white masters the right to whip, at their own discretion, both their white servants and enslaved Africans. However, these same laws declared that white masters could not strip the clothes off of white servants before whipping them, as they could with enslaved Africans. How are we to understand this 'white privilege' of having the right to be whipped with your clothes on, rather than without?

For Thandeka, the "tobacco planters and ruling elite of Virginia raised the legal status of lower-class whites" (p. 43) so they would come to think of themselves as superior to, and hold in contempt, the black people with whom they worked side by side every day; and this "racial contempt would function as a wall between poor whites and blacks protecting masters and their slave-produced wealth from *both* lower-class whites and slaves" (p. 46). Bacon's Rebellion in 1676, among many other instances of cross-racial solidarity, had taught these white masters to fear poor Whites and Blacks banding together (Allen, 2012).

Over time, such laws and tactics by white elites succeeded in persuading white working people to embrace the idea of white supremacy. At the same time, these same laws and tactics reinforced the idea that white elites were better than, were superior to, white folk—white servants remaining vulnerable to being whipped by white masters, but not stripped naked and whipped, is a perfect representation of this.

Within such a scheme and hierarchy, white working people who separate themselves from people of color prove themselves worthy of a few pitiful privileges. Even better for white elites (even worse for the very souls of white folk) is when my people take up the whip against our sisters and brothers of color to prove our worthiness, *when we reduce ourselves to acting as the violent hand of white elites who, in the end, still despise us.*[6] In other words, and to bring this back to why Jack's parents might have been concerned about their son's friendships with two black boys, white adults, especially from lower classes, would do well to make sure that their white children do not identify too closely with, do not have friendships with, do not fall in love with, do not stand in solidarity with people of color, lest these children not grow up to be good white people—exactly because they do not separate themselves from people of color, because they are not white enough.

In sum, for Thandeka, white racial identities emerge in the racial abuse, by white authority, of its own community, with this abuse meted out in intimate relations among family and friends as well as in larger relations constructed in law, policy, and social class. The result is a white racial identity riddled with shame and ambivalence—a white racial identity defined by a desire to reach out beyond the white community and a deep confusion about and fear of this wanting.

★ ★ ★

Religious belief was part of Delores's ambivalence. She was a devout Catholic, and for her that meant that every person was to be treated with dignity. But she also knew that the society she lived in did not treat everyone with dignity; furthermore, she understood that our society was willing to punish those who attempted to protest racial injustice. As Delores said, "Well if it harms somebody else, you should tell"; but then she continued: "What's going to happen to me if I tell? You know, what's going to happen to me if I protest?"

Thandeka's insights help us understand, I think, how the fear that seems so central to white racial identities—as it was with Delores—is often generated *not by negative experiences with people of color or even menacing stereotypes of them, but by white authority figures.* For Delores, the care and support of her white parents and teachers would be risked if she got into trouble protesting. She feared abandonment, being banished—"you do not come home." And all around her was evidence that white police were willing to inflict harm not just on protestors, but even on those just watching—even on those, like Delores, who thought that they could be "innocent bystanders."

I tried to learn more about the 1968 Democratic Convention in Chicago because of how important it was to Delores's story. In one chronology of the events of the convention that I found, the evening of Monday, August 26, was described this way:

> As the curfew approaches, some in Lincoln Park build a barricade against the police line to the east. About 1,000 remain in the park after 11 PM. A police car noses into the barricade and is pelted by rocks. Police move in with tear gas. Like Sunday night, street violence ensues. But it is worse. *Some area residents are pulled off their porches and clubbed. More reporters are attacked this night than at any other time during the week.*
>
> (Blobaum, 2008, my emphasis)

White fear of people of color is generated not just by stereotypes. It is also generated by white violence against its own community, including against its own children and youth. Conscience, friendship and solidarity with people of color, standing too close—these have been and will be punished.

⋆   ⋆   ⋆

Frank pointed to a different sort of fear—the fear of being called a racist—as he talked with me about the protests against proposed immigration laws that occurred across the United States on May 1, 2006, as well as told me about conversations about these protests within his school. This fear was part of only one of the two primary spaces in which he thought white people moved and lived. He characterized this space—the high, "politically correct" one—this way:

> You have to be politically correct about everything. My goodness, if I say the wrong thing or have a thought out loud … you're not allowed to, out loud, question, have a conversation because everyone—"My God, I might get sued, I might lose my job." You would think that people in a break room would be able to have a comfortable conversation about—"This is why I really feel that they're actual illegal aliens. I feel good calling them illegal aliens because they are breaking the law and there should be a consequence. I don't get to break the law"—but you can't have that conversation if you're a white person because people might think I'm a racist. You can see these guys on TV. They're being so cautious about the way they talk because one slip is going to be used against them forever. Everything will come tumbling down so that—the person may not actually be racist. They may just be trying to work through their thoughts but they are not allowed to do that in public.

For Frank, the high space restricted honest exchange. It precluded him from having conversations in which different positions would be expressed and sorted through. The threat of being labeled a racist stifled not just racist talk, but other talk that might not be racist but could be labeled that way.

It is important to note that as there were no teachers or staff of color at his school, Frank was talking about what it is like to talk with *other white people* about immigration and race (except, perhaps, when he supposes that his own experiences are like those of white speakers on TV). That is, when Frank anticipated someone else calling him a racist, he was imagining this being done by another white person. I return to this below.

In consequence of the restrictedness of the high space, certain kinds of talk and ideas and feelings get pushed down into what Frank called a "subculture" or, with reference to a weekly poker game with friends, a "basement culture."

Immediately following the above quote, Frank discussed some of the qualities of this low space:

> I get a lot more leeway to be extreme on different things, no matter what the issue. So, if you push a legitimate conversation that maybe should be more public into that subculture, whether it's on sex or race or whatever, I think people, men especially, but people tend to be a little freer and nastier. Maybe I'm not a racist but in that subculture, I'll go way out on a limb and say some pretty horrible things because I'm being rewarded by other people that are functioning in a subculture mentality.

At first glance, the dominant quality of Frank's subculture seems to be freedom, license. But there was also the sense, here, of group norms that pressed for being "extreme on different things." On the one hand, Frank spoke of "leeway" and the possibility of being "a little freer and nastier." On the other, he spoke of rewards for saying "horrible things" that may or may not be sincere expressions of what a given speaker thought or felt.

I asked Frank if there were regular topics or themes taken up in the basement culture of the weekly poker games. I wasn't necessarily surprised by the themes he mentioned. I was surprised by a rule that had arisen in the group to avoid serious conflict:

> Well, you're going to have sex. ... I'd say in a much more inappropriate, conquest type, that's definitely a topic. Work-type things that you wouldn't normally tell somebody. Race is in there almost all the time. If somebody's having a marital problem ... even that other thing [the protests against proposed immigration laws]. That is going to be right there. "Sons of bitches, if you don't like the country, get the hell out," and then it gets raunchier and worse. ... Political things get talked about. Actually, in my group, you get penalized for talking about politics because that political conversation draws people to damn near fight. So, at a card game, you're penalized. If you make any political statement or take a political side, you have to put up a certain amount of more money into the pot ... because it polarizes people to where they don't want to talk to you ever again.

Sex, work, marriage, and race, along with current topics in the news—for Frank, these were dominant themes taken up in this subculture. I asked Frank for clarification of what he meant by "political conversation" and he pointed to disagreements across conservative and liberal lines. This group of men had learned, over time, that conversations that tapped into such conflicts might get out of hand, and they had instituted a rule against them. If you violated the rule, you threw money into the pot.

These men disagreed on more than politics, but apparently a rule was not necessary for managing those conflicts. Instead, according to Frank, you were supposed to "be quiet" and "just go along." In what follows, Frank once again highlighted how this subculture rewarded talk or performances that belittled and marginalized those not white, not male, not heterosexual—in this case, with a story about a "lesbian Thanksgiving." And toward the end of this part of the interview, Frank named what was a key characteristic or norm of this low space that distinguished it from the politically correct high space and that enabled the sort of talk and laughter found there—*no shaming*:

> What's interesting about that subculture is even if you have a different opinion, you're not going to, you're just going to go along. You're not going to talk about the lesbian Thanksgiving that I went to and the fact that she's not a freak. She's a decent lady, but she's got three kids. But I'm going to tell you how she got the kids because that's a curiously interesting story and it gives me permission to find a way to bash them in [such] a way that you're going to reward me and make me feel good. Same thing goes on with race. ... And I think it goes back to, political issues, people are much more willing to stand up for their political views than they ever would be towards a sexuality issue or a race issue. "Say what you're going to say. I'm just going to be quiet about it." Because if I were to challenge you on that, it's either going to erupt into something terrible, lose a friendship over it or I'm going to make a person feel so horrible. Because of the way it's looked upon, and it's almost like you'd be taking the rules from this politically correct environment and pushing them down into that subculture where, "Gee, now I'm going to shame this guy into complete—," like "How dare you talk like that?"

At least two things here deserve extended comment, and these are developed in the next section. First, I explore how Frank worried about how the basement culture's humor and scapegoating were impacting its members, including himself. Then, I take up the significance, to Frank, of not shaming others in the basement culture and the trouble this created for Frank as he tried to imagine if not antiracist action, then at least what he called a "non-racist" way of living.

★   ★   ★

Frank thought that the woman he knew who was a lesbian and had three kids was a "decent lady" and "not a freak." But he did not tell his friends that or that he and his family spent Thanksgiving with her. He would not be rewarded for sharing such information. Instead, he told what he called a "curiously interesting story," a humorous story about what I assume to be how she became pregnant. It is this performance that results in the subculture rewarding Frank and making him feel good.

Humorous performances that "bash them," that scapegoat others, were valued in this basement culture. Indeed, when I looked back in the interview for when Frank first talked about this subculture, his description mentioned humor and laughter immediately:

> One guy does this great humorous imitation of what he thinks Hmong people must sound like and he can go on and on while people are drinking and playing cards, just a hoot. But you wonder how many times do you have to hear, before you might just actually start to believe it? I know he doesn't have any experiences with them. So, if you were ever to carry on a more "out of basement" type of conversation with him, I would put money on that you would start to hear some things that would trickle into the more adult or more formal conversation that you'd be having. The same kind of perceptions he has of the Hmong culture. "All of them are on welfare, and why do they come here? And all the gangs are from them."

Frank thought that these performances had potential effects on what people believed. He thought that aspects of basement performances might "trickle" into "out of basement" talk, and he wondered how many times you had to participate in such events before you "actually start to believe" what these performances were teaching about scapegoated others. In other words, Frank worried that the language and humor of the basement culture were not just expressions of already-existing racist thoughts and feelings, but that they could produce them. As Frank put it:

> I think even a good person who's probably not racist, but if that's all they have in their toolbox, and you have to take part in those [basement] conversations, eventually they may, over time, become a functioning racist. That does happen. The things you think become the things you say, and the things you say become your habits, and your habits become your character and there's no way around it.

Frank was not just worried about others; he was worried about himself. He was worried about what was in his own "toolbox." Frank wished for a bigger, more expansive world for himself, his friends, his family. Frank hoped that his own children would act differently, be "braver." He hoped that his own children would not stay silent in the face of explicitly racist talk and jokes, as he and his friends often did. He didn't imagine antiracist action, exactly, but he thought that it was possible to register dissent, to not participate, to not just go along:

> The whole goal in raising the children is to try to get them to be a little more comfortable, to be able to talk about the things in the public setting and take that heat, and be a little bit braver when you're out there. Because

if you are a little bit braver when you're in the subculture, you're also going to be a little bit braver to say, "You know what, I'm not going to challenge you on it but I'm not going to take part in it." There's a difference between listening to a guy blow off steam or say a bunch of racial jokes [and] jumping right in there and doing it. There's a difference. "I'm not here to judge you but I don't have to"—the reality is if you say it and think it, eventually it's going to have an impact on how you feel.

Frank imagined his children confronting the same high and low spaces that he did. He thought that participating differently in the low space—being "a little bit braver"—might help you be able to talk about race in the high space and "take that heat." He wanted to preserve a space to "blow off steam," but he thought that it should be possible to be present without "jumping right in there and doing it." Frank was trying to work out a way to follow the norm of not judging or shaming others in the basement culture while also registering disagreement.

My initial interpretation of the rule against talking about politics was that somehow politics inspired more emotion than other topics. But Frank contradicted this—he said that someone could truly have "that same passion" about race "as they do the political stuff. You can just see it in them. They're passionately racist about it."

In relation to politics, the group instituted a rule meant to prevent "something terrible" from erupting. In relation to other potentially divisive topics, it seems that the group was supposed to exhibit self-control. Frank narrated this self-control as "Say what you're going to say. I'm just going to be quiet about it." This silence allowed the group to avoid rupture. It also prevented someone from making "a person feel so horrible" by shaming them. For Frank, shaming others was an aspect of the high, "politically correct environment," not an aspect of the basement culture.

The possibility of being shamed, being accused of being a racist, weighed heavily on Frank—and the accuser might very well be quite racist themself. The image Frank created was of a community with quite a bit of racism that was expressed in the basement culture, but not in the politically correct one. Furthermore, in the politically correct space, anyone, including people Frank himself considered quite racist, might accuse another of being racist, shame them, and diminish their position and worth in the community. In what follows, I was trying to make sense of this situation with Frank. I wondered why racism couldn't be more openly expressed if it was shared by many in the community.

FRANK: I'm thinking I can't even take a chance on looking like I'm racist … you don't want to be the person who gets alienated out.

TIMOTHY: Well, it's interesting because, we're talking about it, simultaneously, that there might actually be a lot of unexamined racism in a community like this, which seems to be like, then, that you could act with impunity, right? If there's all this sort of—

FRANK: Yeah but people are going to want to, publicly, want to adapt. They're going to shame you. They wouldn't want to be around you.

I confess that for a long time I have tended (from my own long-lived, left-leaning way of being) to dismiss comments about 'political correctness' as little more than a repetition, a parroting, of conservative media figures such as Rush Limbaugh. That is, I interpreted political correctness as a site of struggle between Right and Left (see, for example, Fairclough, 2003) and complaints about political correctness as evidence that conservatives did not want to give any credence to the claims of marginalized groups that something important might be going on in patterned ways of doing language and culture—so, these conservatives charged such claims with political correctness and deemed them insignificant, inappropriate, and even antidemocratic.

Frank's comments about political correctness and shaming suggest that something else, or something more, is at stake here. For me, Frank was pointing to the potential for any talk about race to be used in a struggle, *among white people*, over who is and who is not considered a "good" white person. Thandeka (2001) and historian Matthew Jacobson (1998), among others, argue that even as it has always been an advantage to be white in this country, there have also been consequential struggles among different white ethnic groups and social classes over who are deemed worthy and less worthy white people. Political correctness, then, might be more than just an argument between prominent members of the Right and Left (distributed through various media). It seems that this argument provides words (tools? weapons?) that have become part of the struggle, among everyday white people, to determine pecking orders of moral worth.

Alternatively, we could interpret Frank's comments against the backdrop of the consequences of the civil rights movement. Bonilla-Silva (2001, 2003), as mentioned earlier in the chapter, thought that the civil rights movement succeeded in persuading white people they needed to talk differently about race, even as attitudes and beliefs might remain largely unchanged—which is what Frank might have been suggesting when he said that "people are going to want to, publicly, want to adapt." One consequence of this that we see with Frank is that the willingness or ability to perform this talk is used as a way for white people to sort themselves out in relation to each other. This happens on the local scene. Local struggles for acceptance and authority are played out around and through talk about race. It is important to note that this struggle is not limited to one between local conservatives and liberals. For Frank, political correctness was a resource that could be used by anyone, to the point that an extremely racist person might use it against a non-racist or less racist person to put them in their place.

The potential for shaming and loss of standing in the politically correct space encourages white people to hide what they really think about race.[7] For Frank, this seemed to produce a sense of sadness, in part because of the lost opportunity to work through his thoughts and feelings with others. I had asked Frank how he thought his ideas about race had changed over time; his reply was:

> This is probably what most people would say—I want to consider myself to be more tolerant, more open-minded, educated, more compassionate. But I think what most people won't tell you is I still worry that if I don't put thought into that, I, myself, probably have some of those same underlying ideas. Would I laugh at something I probably shouldn't? Am I uncomfortable if I'm in Minneapolis and I see some guys on the street … when I'm driving at night to get something and I drive through a part of town, suddenly all the signs are Chinese and then there's a lot of people on the streets. Why am I terrified when there's thousands of cars, nothing's happening? So I could tell you a whole lot of great stuff, how I feel about myself. Then, still at times I wonder where I am in the world.

Hiding, here, for Frank, seemed related to working to maintain an image of himself to others as non-racist, even as he worried that he might have racist "underlying ideas" and was confused about where he was "in the world." He wanted others to think well of him even if he was not so sure about how he thought of himself. Of course, hiding could take on a more sinister aspect, as when Frank described the hiding engaged in by another man in the community:

> I can tell you about a guy that's extremely racist and you wouldn't hear it in his public talk. I would say you could probably see it in his public action. I would almost guarantee that you would see it, in the position of management, in who he hires, who he doesn't hire. Nothing you could pinpoint but you know it.

For me, this suggests that Bonilla-Silva (2001, 2003) is both right and wrong in his characterization of the new white talk. He's right that white people are hiding. But I think he tends to interpret this hiding *only* in terms of the protection and maintenance of white privilege and supremacy. That is, as white people, we talk in obfuscating ways about race so that everything can just go on as it is, with us in places of privilege relative to people of color.

Frank agrees that polite white talk can hide racism. But he also suggests that white hiding is related to *struggles among white people*, at the local level, for moral worth and standing. Rather than being about (or only about) maintaining white privilege, hiding is often about maintaining status in relation to other white people.

If white people were hiding what they actually thought and felt about race in the politically correct space, then Frank's characterization of the basement culture suggests that it was also not, in the end, a space to honestly express and work through race. The basement culture rewarded extremes, especially ones expressed in humorous performances. After Frank told me about the man he considered "extremely racist," I asked if the basement culture was a place this person could express how he felt. Frank said yes, but he was more interested in the problem the basement culture created for someone who did not think that way:

FRANK: But then you have another person who doesn't think that way who will just go along with it because it's in the subculture and there's not an appropriate place to have that dialogue. ... And then up here [in polite space], this is actually how I am. I'm just not able to talk about what I want to have a conversation about.

TIMOTHY: So, for them, neither place is a place for them to have the conversation, because the subculture isn't the place to talk about it either.

FRANK: No, they don't have it there.

Frank described basement and politically correct spaces in which he could not engage in frank talk about what he thought and felt about race. This produced the need to, at times, hide his ideas, either through silence or through talk that distorted his sincere beliefs but was acceptable in a given space. Frank thought that his thinking about race was stuck because he couldn't sort through conflicting positions with others on important questions and issues. There was disagreement among white people in relation to race, and this disagreement played itself out not just among white people, but also within them. Like Delores, Frank was stuck, conflicted, ambivalent about race.

★   ★   ★

Both Delores and Frank invoked their children as they talked with me about race and about who (and where) they were, as white people, in our society. Frank loaded his hopes for progress on the shoulders of his young children—maybe they, unlike their father, could be "braver;" maybe they could somehow grow up and take the "heat" of confronting our country's racial present and past in high and low spaces. Delores's daughter was already grown, but Delores had feared for her exactly because her daughter seemed to want to be braver. In college, Delores had watched others take that heat, and decades later it still produced fever dreams of police with truncheons and dogs, nightmares of exile, of not being able to go home.

White elites have allowed us to keep our clothes on as they whip us. We are so grateful. We play our part in securing white supremacy through our fear and hiding, our action and inaction.

Notes

1   With Bonilla-Silva, I believe that a color-blind racism is the current racial ideology that sustains racial inequality in the United States. I also believe that his interview studies, along with the work of Frankenberg (1993), are among the most important empirical research we have for making sense of whiteness and race in the United States. However, while Bonilla-Silva (2003) interprets white people's new style of talk—with its long pauses, contradictions, and digressions—as evidence of a straightforward, underlying racism-in-need-of-hiding, I tend to view this talk as the expression of a deeply conflicted, ambivalent white racial self (see also Lensmire and Snaza, 2010).

2   In late August of 1968, the Democratic Party held its national convention in Chicago to nominate its presidential candidate. The convention became the center of a storm of protest, with between 10,000 and 15,000 demonstrators in conflict with 12,000 police and 6,000 National Guard troops. See Blobaum (2008) for a chronology of events leading up to, during, and after the convention.

3   On November 14, 1960, Ruby Bridges, who was six years old, became the first black student at William Frantz Elementary School, an all-white school in New Orleans. She is credited with being the first black student to attend any white school in the South. Norman Rockwell's *The Problem We All Live With* portrays the young Bridges walking between the federal marshals who escorted her into the school (see www.lewisbond.com/rckwellpgs/problem.html for an image of the painting). In 1991, Rodney King, a black taxi driver, was beaten by Los Angeles Police Department officers after being stopped for speeding. The event was videotaped by a bystander. See Gooding-Williams (1993) for a reading of the event against the backdrop of U.S. history and white racism.

4   Tim O'Brien, author of *The Things They Carried*, is actually from Minnesota.

5   I am certainly persuaded by work on how the claim of innocence functions within whiteness to justify white privilege and superiority. Carol Schick and Verna St. Denis (2005), for example, write that "Goodness and innocence are talismans of one's superiority. The claim of innocence acts as both cause and effect: one is produced through innocence as superior; superiority is claimed as a sign of one's innocence" (p. 308; see also Srivastava, 2005).

    However, I believe something different was going on with Delores. Instead of innocence as "goodness" (which Delores often attributed not to white people, but to people of color such as Dr. King and Ruby Bridges), Delores seemed to be trading off a meaning of innocence closer to purity or inexperience—innocent because not involved, not experienced, in the open battles she saw going on between the police and protestors. Of course, Delores eventually questioned whether this sort of innocence—the separateness of an "innocent bystander"—was actually possible, much less desirable.

6   Historian Louis L. Woods II (2015), in a brilliant chapter commenting on Trayvon Martin's murder and exploring how immigrants learn that they can prove that they are worthy of inclusion in the United States by doing violence to black people, writes, "As in joining a gang, assimilating into Whiteness has often required violent displays of racial loyalty" (p. 118).

7   My work on the writing of this book was finished well before Trump had become even a serious Republican candidate for president of the United States, much less elected. Obviously, a footnote is inadequate for commenting on Trump's election in relation to the arguments of my book. I hope that *White Folks* contributes to the efforts of others to understand how he got elected and to imagine antiracist action going forward, but for now, two brief comments. First, Trump is merely the latest in a long and continuous line of race-baiting U.S. politicians. Thandeka (2001) provides a particularly apt example from Wisconsin's past in her discussion of a George Wallace rally in Milwaukee that was part of his 1964 presidential campaign. Thandeka observes that Wallace certainly knew "how to work the fears of a *white* crowd" (p. 88). Second, and in terms of the argument of this chapter, one of the ways that we could understand Trump's campaign is that it unleashed into the mainstream what Frank saw as the basement subculture. This subculture was already in existence, but I share Frank's worry that it not only expresses *already existing* thinking and feeling, but also *produces and encourages* similar thinking and feeling. And while I agree with Frank that the 'shaming' aspect of the higher politically correct space represents a serious problem for people who want to work through confused feelings and unformed thinking about race, Trump and his campaign have made it more legitimate, less shameful, for white people to express and act on the worst of themselves.

3

WE USE RACIAL OTHERS ...

White Americans have, from the first, hopelessly confused the real Negroes
and Indians ... with certain projections of their own deepest minds, aspects of
their own psychic life with which precisely they find it impossible to live.
                                                                —*Leslie Fiedler*

For the four men who are the focus of this chapter—Frank, Robert, William, and
Stan—the creation of their white identities was caught up with real and imagined
racial others. In this, these men were not at all special. Nor was their relative
physical and social isolation from people of color, in Boonendam, Wisconsin,
remarkable. Most white people in the United States live segregated lives, spend
their time at home, at school, at work, at worship, with other white people. And
yet people of color loom large in the creation of white selves.

In what follows, I first sketch an account of the social production of white
racial identity with the help of two scholars who explore just how important
racial others have been for the meaning- and self-making of white people
throughout U.S. history. Then, I turn to the words and stories of Frank, Robert,
William, and Stan in order to deepen and complicate this account and to learn
what these men might teach us about whiteness and white racial identity.

Caveats and fine-tuning are needed, certainly, but literary and social critic
Leslie Fiedler (1964) is correct in my opening epigraph. For these white men, real
and imagined people of color were hopelessly confused, as well as amazingly
significant for their psychic and everyday lives. In the lives of these men, people
of color divided factions of families and churches against one another; for
example, when a son stood against his mother on behalf of a sister who was dating
a man who was Mexican American. People of color were integral to moral

lessons these men learned as boys, including positive lessons about fairness and respect in athletics and negative lessons about hypocrisy, as they listened to their white elders project their own failures and demons onto their Ojibwe neighbors. People of color, imagined and real, helped these men understand themselves and their powers—how smart they were, how good, how tough. People of color helped them position themselves in relation to the racist and democratic meanings and values of their workplaces, community, society, and world.

Indeed, these white men bore witness to Ralph Ellison's (1953/1995) claim—especially if we expand Ellison's focus to include stereotypes of a multiplicity of racial others—that

> It is almost impossible for many whites to consider questions of sex, women, economic opportunity, the national identity, historic change, social justice—even the "criminality" implicit in the broadening of freedom itself—without summoning malignant images of black men into consciousness.
>
> *(1953/1995, p. 48)*

My broadest assertion in this chapter—that real and imagined people of color were central to the ongoing production of these white men's racial identities—cuts across my interviews with these men, cuts across their stories. However, I do not emphasize other commonalities in their words and lives. Instead, their stories are presented as variations on this basic theme.

★　　★　　★

I have referenced Ellison's writings on race in previous chapters, but it is time to explicate his work in more detail. Ellison illuminates how white men have used people of color not only for their labor and economic gain, but also as a cultural and symbolic resource.

Ellison, like Fiedler (1964) in the opening epigraph, thought that stereotypes of racial others were projections. However, Ellison theorized these stereotypes in terms of a larger scapegoating rite or ritual in which white people participated in order to be white. That is, Ellison thought of stereotypes as a particular instance of white people *sacrificing black people*, killing them, symbolically, in order to assure themselves of their own whiteness and superiority. Another instance of this scapegoating ritual was lynching, when black people were literally killed, literally sacrificed, so that white people could go on being white.

For Ellison, scapegoating worked by progressing through three moments: first, the group doing the scapegoating identified with the scapegoat (that is, the scapegoat was a substitute for the group); second, the group separated itself from the scapegoat, declared that the scapegoat was an 'other,' was not them; and finally, the group experienced a renewed sense of unification, was reassured of its identity.[1]

Thus, when Ellison (1986) examined the situation of poor white farmers in the Jim Crow South, he noted that they were "uncomfortably close to Negroes in economic status"; and he thought that they found the possible rewards available to them in America as a land of opportunity "far less inviting than clinging to the conviction that they, by the mere fact of race, color, and tradition alone, were superior to the black masses below them" (pp. 175–176). This conviction, this belief in their superiority, however, was challenged at every moment of every day by the actual material conditions of their lives and by their position at the bottom of the South's white social hierarchy that defined them as "poor white trash" (p. 174). For Ellison, then, these poor Whites needed ways to reassure themselves of their whiteness and their superiority:

> In rationalizing their condition, they required victims, real or symbolic, and in the daily rituals which gave support to their cherished myth of white supremacy, anti-Negro stereotypes and epithets served as symbolic substitutions for the primitive blood rite of human sacrifice to which they resorted in times of racial tension.
>
> *(1986, p. 177)*

Stereotypes were "symbolic substitutions" for a more "primitive blood rite of human sacrifice"—lynching. He even thought that it was fortunate—for Blacks and the nation as a whole—that most of the time stereotypes were enough, that the "Southern rituals of race were usually confined to the realm of the symbolic" (p. 177). When they were not enough, the lynch mob did its work.

Ellison certainly recognized that lynching, by instilling terror into the black community, functioned along with Jim Crow laws and social custom and anti-black stereotypes to reinforce white control and racial hierarchies. But he was also intent on understanding the meaning and function of lynching for white people. For Ellison, white people, especially poor white people, had difficulty denying the basic humanity of black people. But if white people were to recognize this humanity, then white supremacy would need to be dismantled and the social order would need to change. Thus, Ellison (1986) argues, for the lynch mob, blackness was associated with "satanic evil," not only or even primarily because of a Christian tradition that associated darkness with evil, but because blackness "symbolizes all that its opponents reject in social change and in democracy" (p. 178). If, for Fiedler (1964), stereotypes pointed to aspects of white people's "own psychic life with which precisely they find it impossible to live" (p. 117), then what poor white farmers in the South could not live with—when all they really had going for them was their whiteness—was the all too easy recognition of their similarity to, their continuity with, black people.

Ellison had no interest in supporting, even implicitly, the common-sense notion in the United States that it was poor and working white people who were the 'real' racists, allowing higher-classed Whites to congratulate themselves on their racial enlightenment and sophistication. Thus, even as Ellison analyzed the existential situation of poor Whites in the South and their rituals of stereotypes and lynch mobs, he also understood these white people as actors who were taking up a script that was written long before they were born.

The Founding Fathers wrote the original script and were its first and crucial players. Ellison (1986) considered the Constitution a sacred document and a "script by which we seek to act out the drama of democracy, and the stage upon which we enact our roles" (p. 330).

Unfortunately, from the first, the actions of the Founding Fathers clashed with their noble spoken lines. They abandoned the sacred principle of equality. They balked in the face of the economic consequences for them of dismantling slavery, balked in the face of the arduousness and uncertainty of actually attempting to live out democracy. As Ellison put it:

> At Philadelphia, the Founding Fathers were presented the fleeting opportunity of mounting to the very peak of social possibility afforded by democracy. But after ascending to within a few yards of the summit they paused, finding the view to be one combining splendor with terror. ... if there was radiance and glory in the future that stretched so grandly before them, there was also mystery and turbulence and darkness astir in its depths. ... So having climbed so heroically, they descended and laid a foundation for democracy at a less breathtaking altitude, and in justification of their failure of nerve before the challenge of the summit, the Founding Fathers committed the sin of American racial pride.
>
> *(1986, pp. 334–335)*

The Founding Fathers chickened out. They abandoned the principle of equality and blamed their failure of nerve and greed on black people. For Ellison, then, the Founding Fathers were the original scapegoaters, and this act of scapegoating was a gift to the American people that kept on giving.

This was a gift, obviously, with profound, horrific consequences for black people. The Founding Fathers also gave a sickening gift to their fellow white Americans and those of us who followed. Ambivalence, hypocrisy, difficulty in seeing who we really are as white people—these are among our inheritance, what we gained along with thin rationalizations for white privilege. Furthermore, Ellison thought that by scapegoating black people, the Founding Fathers ended up putting race at the very center of the American drama. And because race influenced the

> Ethical sphere no less than the material world—the principle of equality being a command that all men be treated as equals, while some were obviously being designated unequal on the basis of color and race—it made for a split in America's moral identity that would infuse all of its acts and

institutions with a quality of hypocrisy. Worse, it would fog the American's perception of himself, distort his national image and blind him to the true nature of his cultural complexity.

(1986, p. 333)

For Ellison, then, what white people cannot live with is their social role as white people in the American drama, given that playing this role demands the betrayal of the sacred principle of equality. Wanting to believe in America, freedom, and equality, but confronted with the hard work and uncertainty of democracy as well as with massive inequality all around us, we scapegoat and stereotype people of color. As Ellison (1953/1995) wrote, "Perhaps the object of the stereotype is not so much to crush the Negro as to console the white man" (p. 41).

*   *   *

My second theorist of white confusion and projection is Fiedler, who argued that the American Dream, for white men, might have as much to do with a desperate wish for racial reconciliation as it does with economic opportunity. When Fiedler (1964) read nineteenth- and twentieth-century literature and popular culture, he found a consistent theme: a dream or myth of a "Garden of Eden with two Adams" (p. 129). Over and over, our American novels and films featured pairings of a white male and another male of color, expressing what Fiedler called our "national myth of masculine love" (1955, p. 143) and the "white man's dream of reconciliation" (1964, p. 109). Fiedler pointed to Chingachgook and Natty Bumppo in James Fenimore Cooper's *Leatherstocking Tales*, Queequeg and Ishmael in *Moby Dick*, and Twain's Jim and Huck; and later, Sam Feathers and Ike in Faulkner's "The Bear," Chief Bromden and Randle Patrick McMurphy in *One Flew Over the Cuckoo's Nest*, and the characters played by Tony Curtis and Sidney Poitier in the film *The Defiant Ones*.

For Fiedler, this was a sentimental and outrageous dream, a dream with roots in white atrocities against people of color—colonialism and genocide and cultural eradication, slavery and lynching and Jim Crow. It was a dream born of the fear that as white men, we had cut ourselves off, forever, from the love of our brothers. With reference to the white narrator of Melville's *Moby Dick*, Fiedler wrote that:

Ishmael is in all of us, our unconfessed universal fear ... that we may not be loved, that we are loved for our possessions and not our selves, that we are really—alone. ... Behind the white American's nightmare that someday, no longer tourist, inheritor, or liberator, he will be rejected, refused, he dreams of his acceptance at the breast he has most utterly offended. ... Our dark-skinned beloved will take us in. ... He will fold us in his arms saying,

"Honey" or "Aikane"; he will comfort us, as if our offense against him were long ago remitted, were never truly real.

(1955, pp. 150–151)

Fiedler thought that inside us, as white men (and close to this despairing wish for forgiveness), was the fear that what we had done could never be forgiven. We feared that black and Native men must also be dreaming—not of reconciliation, but of revenge. Their dream of revenge is our nightmare, the "black rebellion and red massacre we have portrayed for decades in popular fiction and films" (Fiedler, 1964, p. 116). Fiedler thought that even as this nightmare filled white men with fear, we also wished for this revenge to happen. We longed for an accounting that would finally settle the score.

In sum, Ellison theorized stereotypes as scapegoating rituals meant to secure racial hierarchy and obscure our failure of nerve before the demands of democracy. Fiedler's account of how white men end up confusing real and imaginary people of color is at once as sweeping as Ellison's—extravagant offenses like genocide and slavery put all of this in motion—and, at the same time, intimate. White men fear that our sins and the sins of our fathers might alienate us forever from potential brothers, friends, comrades, and lovers. And so we dream of reconciliation and quake at the terrors we have unleashed and for which we may/must pay.

★   ★   ★

I took up Frank's sense of high and low white spaces in the last chapter. Here, I focus on Frank's discussion of his uncle, Norman. Frank's first description of his uncle was not very positive, and later ones would do little to alter this first impression. Frank said that his uncle was "very alcoholic, hates black people, not sure he likes Catholics too much either." Throughout the interviews, Frank tried to distinguish his father from Norman: "I would see my uncle Norman that would really be hard on some people, and yet my father never modeled that behavior."

In the following, Frank characterized Norman's response to local Ojibwe efforts to claim their fishing rights on nearby lakes and rivers. These rights included taking fish in traditional ways, including spearfishing. Here and in other parts of the interviews, Frank described his uncle's (and his father's) illegal deer hunting and fishing practices and engaged in what seemed to be an imagined dialogue between Norman and himself. Frank was obviously producing this dialogue now, as an adult, but my sense was that he might have wanted to say this to the adults in his life when he was young as he heard their talk and witnessed their actions:

FRANK: They were just really, "Awww, the Indians are stealing. They're drunks. All they're doing is going drunken spearfishing, not doing anything sporting.

And it's a bunch of shit—their culture, they're not the same ones that were here 200 years ago. They should do what we have to do." "OK, well, what do you have to do?" "Well, I have to get up at four in the morning to go out and poach all my deer before the game warden catches me." If you ask them "What do you have to do?" "Well, I have to buy a license and follow all the rules." "Well, no you don't. I've been with you when you've broken all those rules." "But they're not forced to live the life I am." But if he described his life, it wasn't the one he was living. But it's that same attitude. "Everyone should have to be in my hell. They shouldn't get anything better."

TIMOTHY: But you saw this as a kid already.

FRANK: Well, yeah, they were just so obvious. ... And I don't think my dad's way of wrong was quite the level of Norman's level, but then again, I'm trying to justify my father better than my crazy alcoholic uncle. I know I'm doing that because I wonder at times, when those two guys are out, who knows what evil—you know, I don't know what he was doing or shooting and maybe he just left it at Norman's.

According to Frank, Norman denied that the Ojibwe had the right to take fish in traditional ways. His refusal to recognize this right seemed to be grounded, in part, in his belief that these people were not *real Indians* because real Indians had lived "200 years ago." This idea or story—that Native peoples were always already vanishing or always already *gone*—has a long history in our country and has always been useful for easing our conscience when white people forced Native Americans off their land or, as in this case, when we don't want to honor treaties (see Deloria, 1998).

Frank claims to have seen through the lies and hypocrisy of Norman, even as a boy. He wanted to think of his father differently, but Frank recognized that he was "trying to justify" his father and that, in the end, he had little actual knowledge of the extent to which his father differed from Norman in what he was "doing or shooting." Frank saw his uncle breaking rules; he heard him attempt to explain away his behavior; and he heard him, in the same breath, accuse others (in this case, Ojibwe fishermen and their communities) of being morally bankrupt for not following the rules.

Norman scapegoated people of color. However, even if, as Ellison argued, this scapegoating enabled Norman to think of himself as superior to them, it also seemed to cost Norman, seemed to cause him psychic pain. Frank said that Norman struggled with alcoholism and depression, and he thought that Norman's time in Vietnam and the death of his brother there contributed to his difficulties:

I think he spent seven years in Vietnam. He decided to come back and then another brother went over. His name was Eric and he got killed and then Norman went into the psychiatric hospital, spent a year there and now, to this day, he drinks heavily. But when he's drinking—I've experienced this—he's broken down and cried, "I think I might have been the guy that assassinated Martin Luther King. I'm not sure." He'll have moments, but then he'll be this giant, generous guy. He'll pick up a guitar and just play very—kind of renaissance in those areas.

Obviously, much could (and should) be made of Norman's worry when he was drunk that he may have assassinated Dr. Martin Luther King Jr. Many interpretations, from diverse disciplines and perspectives, could be generated. The one developed below proposes that Norman, at such moments, intuited something important about the constitution of his own white racial identity.

In *Rabelais and his World*, Russian philosopher Mikhail Bakhtin (1984) explored folk humor and popular festivals in the Middle Ages and during the Renaissance because he saw in them lessons for how to oppose an oppressive social order and official ideology. Bakhtin thought that official truth was held in place by fear. Consequently, he was interested in how that fear might be lifted or countered. He theorized that feasting—sitting with friends, eating, drinking, laughing—might provide occasions for fearlessness and that, with this fearlessness, counter-truths might be perceived and expressed.

There is an inverted feasting here with Norman, one with drinking and tears. However, these tears and drinking appear to have enabled moments of truth-telling.

As explored in the previous section, Ellison (1986) thought that the sorts of stereotypes Norman espoused about black and Native peoples were "symbolic substitutions" for a more "primitive blood rite of human sacrifice" (p. 177). Furthermore, Ellison argued that such scapegoating rituals were crucial to the creation and maintenance of white people's sense of themselves as white and American. Norman's fear that he had killed Dr. King, then, seems an uncanny recognition of the connections Ellison draws between stereotyping and blood rites and identity. In other words, the truth Norman expressed at these moments was that his identity, in some profound way, was dependent on killing people of color.

★   ★   ★

Robert was an educator and a basketball coach. Two interrelated themes are developed with Robert's interviews. The first is that people of color often became the focus of conflict within this white community. Stated differently, there was not an agreed upon, monologic word or perspective about race in this community. The second theme is that Robert's physical and moral development as a boy was wrapped up with people of color, even though he had little contact with them when he was young.

Experiences with people of color increased for all of these men as they grew older, both because of the expansion of activity and interaction that comes with becoming an adult and because of demographic shifts that included Hmong and Mexican Americans joining their community. These experiences were often characterized by conflict, which pointed not only to enduring racism within their local community, but also to *conflict within the white community itself.* Thus, Robert resigned as the coach of a nearby city's high school basketball team after the ongoing criticism of him by white parents—criticism that started when he suspended a white player for calling the only black player on the team a racial epithet (*the* racial epithet). In addition, Robert described contentious debates within his Lutheran church over whether it should sponsor and support Hmong immigrants to the area (as did William, discussed below).

Robert told about arguments made by church members in support of sponsoring Hmong immigrants, including ones based in Christian commands to love and care for those in need and ones based on the idea of a debt that they had to pay as U.S. citizens for the Hmong's help during the Vietnam War. (In the end, his church did sponsor and support Hmong families who settled in the area.) Robert also recounted how church members opposed to sponsoring Hmong immigrants talked about their opposition. I asked Robert if he thought that church members who opposed sponsoring Hmong immigrants said what they actually thought or if there were things left unsaid:

ROBERT: I think people were very guarded about saying that in front of people in the church and if they would say anything at all, it would be to the extent of "Well, our job as Christians, first of all, take care of our own. There are many people in our community that need our help first."
TIMOTHY: And "our own" would literally be like the parish?
ROBERT: Parish inside of a circle of a community inside of a circle of the county area and, therefore, "You're excluded." So, people consoled themselves in the fact that—the only way of justifying, saying that I'm not prejudiced. I think there was tremendous prejudice within the Lutheran church, who was really responsible for bringing them here. ... It wasn't openly expressed that way. People had very hidden agendas for the reasons that they shouldn't come, that we should not be sponsoring. I just think it was all race-based.
TIMOTHY: But you didn't hear that. It was just sort of like, or that wasn't said, that "These people are inferior" or undeserving or anything like that and that it was more that "It was going to put a drain on us," but it also sounds like "They're not us," right?
ROBERT: "They're not us. Take care of our own first." Which is kind of a nice way of saying "I'm prejudiced."

We should not be surprised about the unspoken racism that Robert reports, nor that other white people argued for supporting Hmong families on moral and political grounds. Both groups attempted to use a Christian command about caring for others as part of their arguments. The difference, of course, rested on who was to be included within the circle of the church's responsibility: Who is "our own"?

A crucial point here (and one that is often ignored when we conceptualize antiracist efforts in school, university, and religious settings) is that the white community is often divided about race. Furthermore, as noted in the previous chapter, this division works itself into individual white people, who are often conflicted or ambivalent in relation to people of color. This will become more evident in the discussion of William, below.

In relation to Robert, a perhaps surprising aspect of his discussions about race is just how important people of color—specifically, professional athletes—were to his physical and moral development and identity. From an early age, Robert was a serious athlete, and he told about the considerable labor he put into making his body able not only to perform successfully in competition, but also to imitate the arm motion and leg kick of a favorite professional baseball pitcher or the jump shot of a favorite basketball player:

ROBERT: The San Francisco Giants had this Black Hispanic player, Juan Marichal; he had this big leg kick and my brother and I would always pitch to each other. One of us would be Juan and the other one would be the catcher—that big leg kick. And Roberto Clemente, oh my gosh I just loved watching him play. In basketball, I was a huge Knicks fan because I really loved watching Walt Frazier play. Willis Reed—there was another player called Earl Monroe, Earl the Pearl—when those guys, in '69 I think they won, I idolized those guys. The only guy I would want to be other than those guys was Jerry West; he is the insignia on the NBA thing. So, really influential and trying to model how they would play. Trying to shoot like Walt Frazier. He always had his ball way up above his head and kind of back. Those things, those traits, certainly young kids are very impressionable, myself being one of them, would constantly try to emulate those characteristics.

TIMOTHY: Were there other things you remember yourself trying to do or be like? Let's try to figure out like how this—one of the ways that this influenced us was we tried to make our bodies move like these guys. You mentioned the pitcher, the high kick, shooting the ball a certain way.

ROBERT: Football, the Rams used to have Deacon Jones and Merlin Olsen and Rosey Grier, the guy that jumped on Sirhan Sirhan, and my brother and I used to always emulate the front four. I think they were called the 'fearsome foursome,' and I can remember being in the living room and we'd stuff our shirts with pillows and you'd do that stuff. Baseball? Willie Mays was one of the greatest. I can remember him making that over the shoulder catch. Not live, I think he made it in the late '50s, but I remember seeing it played over and over again and oh, man, I would idolize just the way he would play. So, they just had a huge impact on who you tried to be and what you tried to make of yourself.

Robert was attempting to embody particular ways of moving and being as an athlete, and his models for this embodiment came largely from people of color. (Of the ten athletes Robert mentioned by name, only two—Jerry West and Merlin Olsen—were white.) Furthermore, this embodiment extended beyond sports and physical coordination. Robert also talked about how important it was for his emerging understanding of concepts such as respect and fairness to see people of color and white people competing honorably, together, in athletics. His education about race took place largely in relation to athletics:

> I think as we grew up, very seldom did we talk about acceptance of other races [in school]. Curriculum was so different. You didn't have classes in guidance. If it was addressed, it may be addressed in Sunday school. So, personally I think I learned a lot about racism and other races being accepting through sports, through watching it on TV, through watching people shake hands after a good game, through seeing other races work together in all sports. Seeing black announcers for the first time. And especially seeing that black athletes could rise above and really soar and stand out and "Hey, I want to be like that." So that taught you that it's okay to be like that person, that person can be someone you can accept.

There are certainly limits to what young boys could learn about race and racism through athletics, but we should not ignore what Robert said here and in other parts of his interviews. Robert read biographies and autobiographies of his favorite athletes, and consequently he learned about and had to try to make sense of the racism and death threats that Hank Aaron faced as he chased Babe Ruth's home run record in baseball. Athletics, for Robert, was not only the source of scenes for the display of physical skill, but also moral dramas which taught him about intolerance and that it was "okay" to accept and emulate people of color. And as Robert noted, it was not as if such topics were being taken up in school.

In the following, Robert expressed his admiration for the combination of athletic prowess and social grace that he thought baseball player Lou Brock embodied. It does not seem a stretch to draw a line, even if a long and tangled one, between what Robert learned with and from people like Lou Brock and his later decision as a coach to suspend a white basketball player for mistreating a black teammate (whatever the trouble this caused for him in his white community). Robert also recalled his surprise as a young man when he walked alongside Brock before an all star game and discovered that he was now, somehow, as "big" as one of the black athletes he had looked up to for so long:

I remember, I would have been about 16, the last time the Brewers had that all star game, 1975. My friend and I and my dad and brother went down to the all star game, and it was really hard to get tickets so we were sitting up in the nosebleed seats in the upper deck. But we got down there really early, purposely, because we wanted to see the players walk in. All the star athletes, especially Lou Brock and Bobby Mercer from the Yankees, they were let off and then they walked from their limo or cab in. It was so cool walking next to Lou Brock—here's this little guy that you were just as big as—and he was just phenomenal. What a thrill that was just to listen to him talk. You didn't have to say anything, just listen to how he would interact with people around him.

Robert told a story, here, of overcoming social and physical separation. Lou Brock had been distant from Robert, someone glimpsed on television or imagined while reading the sports section of the newspaper. Even during the all star game, he would be far away (though closer) as Robert and his friend and his father and brother watched from the "nosebleed seats in the upper deck."

But Robert was waiting outside the stadium, early, before the game. And then, for a brief moment, he got to walk with Lou Brock, got to be close to him. Being this close, Robert realized that this man he had looked up to was the same size as him. Robert was quiet. He was thrilled, content just to listen to Lou Brock and be close to him.

What is Robert's story—a story about baseball and race and being, finally, *close*—if not what Fiedler (1955) called our "national myth of masculine love" (p. 143)?

★   ★   ★

William was the first person I interviewed. And although I had already done a great deal of work to get ready for this project, I was quite nervous about talking with him. This was more than the usual sort of worry about whether things would go well. There remained within me, I think, some doubt about whether the project could even be done. I hadn't lived in Boonendam for decades—would these people actually talk to me? About race and racism?

We had agreed to do the interview in the early afternoon. I drove to William's home and he invited me into the kitchen, where I spoke with his wife, Riley, and him about the last time they had seen my parents.

Then William talked with me. About race and racism. I remain grateful to him for this.

We sat at the long kitchen table, side by side. The interview was interrupted a few minutes after we started by two men who talked with William out on the porch for close to a half hour. When William came back, he explained that he was in the process of allowing a company to mine sand from some of his property.

He said, "I'm not about bludgeoning the land, but farming is a hard way to make a living."

William and his family owned a small farm, and like many small farmers, their economic situation was precarious. They had inherited the farm from his parents and had been running it for over 15 years, but William was not sure that they were going to make it. Finances were tight.

William belonged to a different Lutheran church than Robert, but his church had also decided to sponsor Hmong families and he agreed with this decision. And like Robert, he was very aware of racism in his own community.

In fact, his knowledge about racism in Boonendam and nearby Wisconsin cities seemed to lead William toward a further stereotyping of black people. He reasoned that the racism of white people, the absence of an established black community, and a depressed local economy would make the area a difficult one for black people to live in. And, therefore, he thought that the few black people who did live in the area must be selling drugs—why else would they be here? He reported not thinking about black people this way when he visited large cities, such as Milwaukee, or when he and his family had taken a vacation to Florida. William's perceptions of black people shifted according to place.

Of the four men, William seemed the most intensely conflicted, the most ambivalent, in relation to race. This was all very personal and close to him. William recounted how his sister had started living with a black man and how, after initially being on friendly terms and having his sister and her boyfriend over to his house, William gradually became worried that the two of them had become addicted to drugs. When his sister, out of the blue, asked his mother for thousands of dollars from his mother's savings, William persuaded his mother not to give his sister any money:

WILLIAM: Boy, then the roof blew off when she told my sister that no money was coming, and we've been called bigots ever since.
TIMOTHY: By her?
WILLIAM: By her. She's told other people that and it hurts and it's not true. I really resent my sister for—"Why are you saying that? You know better. We were brought up all the same out here." I don't understand what happened. If she was a user herself for a while and her brain was toasted or what, but—
TIMOTHY: It seems like very little of this has to do with her boyfriend at all.
WILLIAM: It doesn't have to do with him at all. The only thing it has to do with him or the race thing is that she's using it against us, saying we're racist.

William described, similarly to Frank in the last chapter, how an accusation of racism could be part of a struggle among white people—in this case, a conflict within his own family. His sister's accusation seemed to hurt William profoundly, and I think this was exactly because he was ambivalent, conflicted, inside. Not only did William know about the racism of others, he felt it inside himself.

However, he did not want to feel that way. With considerable candor, William used the interview to articulate to himself and me why he felt the way he did about black people:

WILLIAM: I think what scares me about black people in general is that I think they're very street smart as a race, because a lot of them have been from inner cities or a generation back was from inner cities, had to scrape and scrimp to make, just to eat, and they ended up being very street smart. I mean a lot of blacks are poor. That's not an opinion. That's a fact, and I guess I always figure if you're street smart, then you've probably got a knife on you some place. You probably know all kinds of moves to put somebody on the ground if need be, and that's something that strikes fear in me. Isn't that logical? To me, it is. I always think of them as street smart.

TIMOTHY: Well, we can both mull that over—

WILLIAM: I mean me, being out on this farm, I think of myself as dumb as far as knowing the ins and outs of living in the city. Why wouldn't I be? It's the same as why wouldn't they be smart about it, why wouldn't I be naïve about it. I think it's legitimate and I think it's a reason we distrust them. It's really not about race per se. It is but it isn't. It is because I think blacks in general have those street smarts. Then again, it's not just that they're black, I'm afraid of what they all know how to do or how to hurt me or whatever they needed to—not necessarily want to but—I know I wouldn't want to fight many or any of them one-on-one because I think I'd lose.

TIMOTHY: I think that you're getting to something there. This all gets so mixed up together, it's so hard to sort through what—

WILLIAM: When you think of having a fight in Boonendam, it doesn't involve having a knife, right? It involves somebody usually giving someone a fist in the chops or you're rolling around on the floor or whatever. When I think of fighting with a black person, I almost always see a knife.

In William's imagination, he pictured himself as a poor white man in a fight with a poor black man. Thandeka (2001) would argue that William saw himself exactly how white elites have always hoped he and other hard-working white men would see themselves—as pitted against people of color in a struggle for scarce resources rather than as in conflict with white elites.

In the above, William seems, at times, to want to avoid stereotyping black people. His use of "black people in general" and "blacks in general" could be interpreted as the attempt to recognize that not all black people are the same. But despite these gestures, the overall impression is one in which "we," meaning white people, are different from and fearful of "them," meaning black people.

Although William stereotyped black people around the notion of "street smarts," it was not done with reference to biological or genetic causes. The causes, here, are sociological and economic.[2] The violence and competence that William feared in black men were born of necessity—for William, they have been and are poor and they have had to struggle to survive. When he talked of these men hurting him, William said that they "needed" to do this, not that they wanted to.

If how William thinks and feels about black people was grounded, in part, in stereotyping them as "street smart," then we should acknowledge that William did not make this image up out of nothing. Indeed, it is a pervasive, durable, stereotypical image of black men, one already well established in American literature by the early 1900s when Sterling Brown (1933) named it the "Brute Negro" stereotype.[3] It is a stereotypical image *celebrated* by one of the leading left-leaning, white writers and intellectuals of the twentieth century, two-time Pulitzer Prize-winning author Norman Mailer.

The difference between William and Mailer is that Mailer, in his essay "The White Negro", idolized black men for their street smarts. Indeed, he and other hipsters wanted to *be* this sort of black man, wanted to be *white Negroes*.[4] The same violence and ability to survive that William feared was what the hipsters and Mailer wished to embody themselves. Mailer's reading of black men's existential situation and their responses to it led him to the same stereotypical image as William, except that Mailer added some jazz and sex. Here is Mailer:

> Knowing in the cells of his existence that life was war, nothing but war, the Negro (all exceptions admitted) could rarely afford the sophisticated inhibitions of civilization, and so he kept for his survival the art of the primitive ... relinquishing the pleasures of the mind for the more obligatory pleasures of the body, and in his music gave voice to the character and quality of his existence, to his rage and the infinite variations of joy, lust, languor, growl, cramp, pinch, scream and despair of his orgasm. For jazz is orgasm.
>
> *(1959, p. 341)*

As with William, here is the same ineffectual gesture towards not wanting to stereotype black people: "all exceptions admitted." Here is the same reduction of black men to dangerous bodies (and a reduction of the most sophisticated music of our continent to a spurt of emotion). William feared the black men he imagined this way, feared that they would win if he had to fight them. Mailer understood this fear, wanted, himself, to inspire this fear in others:

> Since the Negro knows more about the ugliness and danger of life than the white, it is probable that if the Negro can win his equality, he will possess a potential superiority, a superiority so feared that the fear itself has become the underground drama of unforeseeable consequences. Like all conservative political fear it is the fear of unforeseeable consequences, for the Negro's

equality would tear a profound shift into the psychology, the sexuality, and the moral imagination of every white alive.

(1959, p. 356)

On this last point about white fear of "unforeseeable consequences," Mailer was right and continues to be right. In this, his analysis was quite close to that of Ellison (1953/1995), who thought, as noted earlier, that it was "almost impossible" for white people to think about almost any serious issue in our country "without summoning malignant images of black men into consciousness" (p. 48). However, Ellison refused to stereotype black people, even when that stereotype might, in some twisted way, suggest their superiority.

William and Mailer, for all their talk about "street smarts" and fearsome black men, were not in the end actually talking about these men. They were talking about themselves. They were using stereotypical renderings of black men to express their own fears and desires *as white men* in our racist and stratified U.S. society.

★   ★   ★

Stan, with his wife and children, ran a larger dairy farm than William's. Their financial situation was better, though Stan felt that as farmers they were caught between, on one side, economic pressures to create bigger and bigger farms and, on the other, increased environmental concerns and regulations that came with bigger farms. Stan despaired that there would not be enough money in farming for his daughter or son to take it up and that Stan and his wife would eventually have to sell a farm that had been in his family for over 100 years.

If one of the problems being explored in this chapter is how imagined and real people of color function in the creation of white racial selves, then Stan did not exactly get off to a good start as a young boy. When asked if he could remember the first time that he realized he was white or that being white somehow mattered to the situation he was in, Stan told about how his mother scared his siblings and him into behaving when they went to the annual county fair:

> I guess that's a tough one because I can remember my first time actually seeing a black person was at the Purgatory County Fair. ... Because my mom would scare the living shit out of us. Give us $5 and told us if we didn't behave—she'd point and say "See that big black man over there? He'll take you." That's what she would say. We'd never seen a black person before in our life. We didn't know if they were good, bad. We didn't know anything about them. ... What's funny about that, when my dad and his brothers would talk, their parents, I guess—back in those times and Gypsies used to travel through here on a regular basis. Well, their moms and dads used the Gypsy scare. If you didn't behave, the Gypsies

were going to take you. They had the scare factor they had to throw into you. Basically, that happened the first time.

Stan thought that this particular othering of a black man at the county fair was a reworking of an older stereotype in this area's Polish and German communities: the thieving Gypsy (where the thieving included children). Stan's mother had pointed at a black man at the fair and rendered him a fearful character who would take misbehaving children away from their parents. (Stan's mother had also told him that if this happened, she would not try to get Stan back.)

He told this story as a humorous one, and it was continuous with other stories Stan told about his mom, who often came off as intolerant and prejudiced in his stories. Thus, Stan also told about his sister who, at the time of the interviews, was dating a Mexican American man who also worked on Stan's farm. Stan's mother had asked Stan to intervene in the situation and demand that his sister stop dating this man. Stan refused, saying that his sister should be able to date who she wanted to.

Stan seemed less conflicted than William. He said that he tried to be open to people who were different from him. This commitment seemed to have some purchase on his action. Stan said that he had fired a white man who worked for him when this man started harassing a co-worker because he was Mexican American. Stan believed that TV and other media had a big role in spreading stereotypes about people of color and that eventually, with constant repetition, white people believed these stereotypes. When I asked him why he did not believe these stereotypes, he theorized that it had to do with his own experiences being overweight. Stan even referred to the prejudice he faced for being overweight as "racism":

> See, I feel I have more open-mindedness than the average guy because there was racism towards me being overweight all my life. I had to be funnier in school. I had to be more outgoing to have friends. Otherwise, people ignored me. So, I can see where all this shit starts. People didn't judge me by my intelligence. I was just a fat kid. That's how it always was and that's just a cruel part of this world.

Stan traced his desire to be racially tolerant to his experiences being "just a fat kid." These experiences, he said, helped him "see where all this shit starts."

His comment that others did not judge him by his intelligence suggests that the link he was making between racism and prejudice against him for his weight had to do with how racist thought connects the *surface* and *depth* of a person. One of the key ways that racism works ("where all this shit starts") is by persuading people that something essential, something *deep*, can be intuited about others from the color of their skin, from their *surface*.[5] Stan's own experiences of being judged by how he looked, then, helped him understand (and reject) this aspect of racist thought.

Stan wanted to be judged by his intelligence rather than by how he looked. There is an echo here of Dr. King's "I have a dream" speech in which he called forth a nation in which his children would "not be judged by the color of their skin, but by the content of their character." Later in the interview, Stan made explicit reference to King and spoke of the deep respect he had for him and other black leaders of the struggle for civil rights. Just as Stan wanted to be recognized for his intelligence, he recognized and emphasized the intelligence of these black leaders.

What follows is taken from a longer discussion about the causes of inequality. Stan believed that white discrimination was a major factor, but he also believed that black people shared some of the blame. He cited comedian and actor Bill Cosby for the claim that the current generation of black people was not doing enough to address their situation.[6] In the middle of this discussion, Stan went on a sort of reverie about civil rights leaders of the past. The scene Stan narrated was a nighttime one, one of dreams and nightmares. He was unable to sleep. He was watching TV:

STAN: I watch a lot of documentaries because I don't sleep, so I watch a lot of that stuff on the Discovery Channel and the History Channel and all that. When we went through the time with Martin Luther King, the blacks, I think—there was true racism then. People just didn't want them in this country. But look how well they were dressed and look how well those guys were educated, the ones that were fighting. … My God, when you watch those old tapes, Martin had very well-educated—and the same with the Black Panthers. They had a very well-educated group of people. … It seems to me that you see less and less of the well-dressed black man out there. That's the way I see it, I don't know.

TIMOTHY: Well, I think if you tried to do a survey of what the media image is, I think that you're right.

STAN: I told you this in the first—the media is actually the one that causes the racism. How many times do you see a story about a well-dressed Black or Indian or whatever on the TV? It's all about drive-by shootings, selling dope, and they're just branding and branding and branding these people. And what you see on the TV is what's going to sink in to your head.

Stan said that the media were "branding" men of color. It seems safest to assume that Stan meant 'brand' as describing someone or something as bad. However, given Stan's concerns to distinguish surface from depth, as well as his ideas about how media such as TV influence thought, it is possible that he was invoking other meanings. Perhaps Stan's repetition of "branding" three times was not only for emphasis, but because the word also suggested marking/burning the skin or all the ways that companies work to create a recognizable and desirable 'brand' for their consumers.

As with William, Stan did not need to do much work to *imagine* dangerous black men—they were everywhere on his TV. But he could find other black men there, too, late at night when he could not sleep.

Stan did not have a lean, athletic body like Robert. When Robert disciplined himself toward athletic prowess and social grace, he dreamed of the bodies and movements of his favorite black and brown athletes. Robert had the sort of body to make this dreaming and moving plausible. Stan dreamed, instead, of being judged by his intelligence. If Dr. King was at the center of a nightmare for Frank's uncle, Norman, then for Stan, King was a companion in a dream of mutual recognition. Stan dreamed the "white man's dream of reconciliation" (Fiedler, 1964, p. 109).

These interviews were conducted in the spring of 2006. Maybe I should not have been surprised, then, in the fall of 2008—as I drove through the Wisconsin countryside, through Purgatory County, on my way to my parents' house in Boonendam, Wisconsin, the town where Stan and William and Robert and Frank lived—that it seemed like there were more Obama than McCain signs on the lawns and in the fields.

Obviously, the 2008 election was about more than race.

Obama took 54 percent of the vote in Purgatory County to McCain's 45 percent. The vote was divided, like Frank, Robert, William, and Stan and their community. But there must have been enough white men, like Stan, who dreamed of being accepted by, imagined reconciliation with, a well-dressed, educated black man.

★ ★ ★

U.S. society remains white supremacist in its structures and practices, notwithstanding the election (and re-election) of our first black president. Individual white racism flourishes, whatever the new, color-blind race talk that grew up in response to the civil rights movement. My emphasis on complexity at the core of white racial selves is not meant to distract from these realities.[7]

However, we often assume that since white people lead segregated lives, people of color are not present in, are not fundamental to, those lives. But they are. Stan longed for intelligent communion with black men; William feared them and mourned that his sister thought him a racist; Robert trained his body to move like the brown and black athletes he idolized, and he watched in dismay as his religious community fought over whether or not Hmong immigrants were within its circle of responsibility, whether they were "us" or "them"; and Frank's uncle, Norman, tried desperately to reassure himself of his own superiority by scapegoating Ojibwe people, as his young nephew looked on in perplexity and shame and lost his innocence. People of color are central to the drama of white lives.

The subject of the dream is the dreamer—this is what novelist Toni Morrison concluded, in her William E. Massey Sr. Lectures in the History of American

Civilization,[8] from her attempt to make sense of how white authors of the American literary canon were using black characters and blackness in their novels. What Morrison (1992) calls the "Africanist presence" or "persona" in these novels had little to do with black people or black culture, but everything to do with who white people were or wished they might be. Morrison wrote:

> As a writer reading, I came to realize the obvious: the subject of the dream is the dreamer. The fabrication of an Africanist persona is reflexive; an extraordinary meditation on the self; a powerful exploration of the fears and desires that reside in the writerly conscious. It is an astonishing revelation of longing, of terror, of perplexity, of shame, of magnanimity.
>
> *(1992, p. 17)*

Frank, Robert, William, and Stan help us realize that white people are always already in relationship to people of color (even if imagined) and always already *know* them. These relationships and knowledge are often rooted in projection and scapegoating, but recognizing stereotypes and dreams of reconciliation as projections—as tangled up in our guts and hearts (not just our heads), as something we *need* to go on living in a violent and unjust U.S. society with a violent and unjust past—helps us better understand why they are so tenacious.

It also creates a space for us to consider the emotional costs of scapegoating and stereotypes for white people. This is not meant to ignore the oppression, misery, and death that scapegoating and stereotypes have produced and continue to produce for people of color. But we also need to come to grips with the sort of emotional distress and confusion that Norman, Frank, and William have experienced. There are costs associated with what Ellison (1953/1995) sees as white Americans' wretched and continual need for reassurance of their own superiority—exactly because white people also know that we are not actually superior.

Longing, terror, perplexity, shame, magnanimity. The subject of the dream is the dreamer.

Notes

1 See Eddy (2003) for a helpful discussion of this aspect of Ellison's work.

2 Of course, this does not mean that such notions were not lurking close by. As Stuart Hall put it in his famous lecture entitled "Race: The Floating Signifier" (Media Education Foundation, 1997), "The biological, physiological, and genetic definition, having been shown out the front door, tends to slide around the veranda and back in through the window."

3 Whatever earlier and other sources William might have encountered, he would have certainly experienced this stereotypical image in the national media as a young man given that an important part of the Reagan Administration's War on Drugs was

propagating the image of the black male as a criminal—see Michelle Alexander's (2010) *The New Jim Crow: Mass Incarceration in the Age of Colorblindness.*

4   Fiedler (1964) thought that Mailer's essay should be interpreted in terms of the older white American dream of chaste love between white man and black; only, here, that union gave birth to a male child, a white Negro.

5   Dyer (1997) argues that race and racism are always about bodies. White people obviously have bodies, but Western thought posits that these bodies, unlike the bodies of racial others, are animated from the inside by an ennobling *spirit*: "The white spirit organizes white flesh and in turn non-white flesh and other material matters: it has *enterprise*. Imperialism is the key historical form in which that process has been realized" (p. 15).

6   Cosby had, at a 2004 meeting commemorating the fiftieth anniversary of *Brown v. Board of Education* in Washington, D.C., made a series of comments that were quite critical of poor black people and that sparked an ongoing controversy. Cosby eventually published a book with Alvin Poussaint, in 2007, that reiterated this message of black responsibility.

7   Nor is it meant to suggest that conflict and ambivalence cannot coexist perfectly well with white supremacy. In fact, complexity and ambivalence are what we would expect within a system that attempts to rationalize violent conditions (Deliovsky, 2010).

8   Morrison's (1992) lectures were later published as *Playing in the Dark: Whiteness and the Literary Imagination.*

4

... AND HOPE AND STUMBLE

When Delores's daughter and son were young, she took them to get their pictures taken. Her children had not had many experiences with people of color, and the photographer was black:

> I had the experience of taking my children, when they were preschoolers, to one of those photographers set up at Penney's or Kmart or wherever. And the photographer took the pictures and was showing us the proofs, and he was African American and my daughter asked why his hands were dirty. Right away, he tried to cover for me and said, "That's okay. I'm not offended." And I took his hand and said, "His hands aren't dirty. He's African American and this is his name," and I gave her his name. But I thought, for me, if she thought that was dirt—and she was old enough to know that I don't go for dirt—that, no, his hands are not dirty. I will touch his hands.

In previous chapters, I have explored aspects of white people's fear in relation to people of color, but in this story, Delores's interaction with a black photographer was not characterized by fear, but something more like politeness and, perhaps, even mutual, genuine decency. The photographer tried immediately to "cover" for Delores, to help her avoid feeling embarrassed because her daughter asked why his hands were dirty. Delores responded by holding the photographer's hand and telling her daughter his name.

Delores's young daughter had regarded the photographer's hands as "dirty", and as psychiatrist and social critic Joel Kovel (1970) reminds us, dirt or, more correctly, a *fantasy about dirt* plays an important part in white people's racial imaginary. Kovel notes that:

Every group which has been the object of prejudice has at some time been designated by the prejudiced group as dirty or smelly or both. ... The English upper classes regarded the English middle and lower classes as dirty ... and if the lower classes had "Untouchables," as in India, they would have doubtless exercised the same privilege over the lowliest as did the various castes within Indian culture. Indeed, lowest in social scale connotes the idea of dirtiest and smelliest, and untouchability sums up all these concepts in the framework of aversion.

(1970, pp. 81–82)

Clearly, Delores understood this fantasy of dirt, and she took action to disrupt or disable the development of this fantasy in her daughter. It is significant—and an almost perfect counter to the aversion, the turning away from, that the fantasy of dirt encourages—that the crucial actions for Delores were to hold the photographer's hands and to tell her daughter his name. I interpret the latter as an act meant to individuate this man, to not allow him to be reduced to an anonymous representative of an undesirable group. As for the former, Delores said that her three-year-old daughter was old enough to know that she (Delores) did not "go for dirt." Delores was anxious for her daughter to know that this man was not dirty. As she said later, "When [my daughter] made that comment, it's just that she was wrong and I didn't want her thinking there were dirty people in the world."

Delores was trying to help her daughter become the kind of white person who recognized the fundamental equality of all peoples—that there were no "dirty people in the world." But it is significant that she *used* this black person to do this.

For we could read Delores's story differently. In this alternative reading, Delores was presumptuous. She took the man's hands without asking him whether or not he wanted to be touched by her, whether or not he wanted to participate in this 'teachable moment' for her daughter on how to read other people's skin. Delores was focused on her daughter, not the man. She used the man as little more than a prop to teach her daughter a lesson. In this second reading, Delores's story provides just another example of how serviceable people of color have been for white people, provides more evidence (as if it were needed) for Ralph Ellison's (1953/1995) claim that we should "view the whole of American life as a drama acted out upon the body of a Negro giant who, lying trussed up like Gulliver, forms the stage and scene upon which and within which the action unfolds" (p. 28).

For me, each of these two divergent readings—this is a story about mutual, cross-racial civility and a mother's action meant to immobilize a powerful racist fantasy; no, this is a story about a white woman conscripting a black man for her own purposes—each is true. In earlier chapters, as in the second reading of Delores's story, I focused on how white people have exploited people of color not just by stealing their land and labor, but by using them symbolically, ritually, in order to work out who we are, in order to create ourselves and our children as white. In this chapter, and as in the first reading of Delores's story, I focus more on how experiences narrated by Erin, Libby, and Frank might suggest something hopeful, how they might open out into something better.

Inspired by the Reverend Thandeka's (2001) interviews with white people, I had asked Erin and Libby and the rest to tell me about the first time that they realized they were white. And as with Thandeka's informants, most shared negative or disturbing experiences—Stan's story about how his mother had used a black man at the Purgatory County Fair to scare Stan into good behavior was, perhaps, the most dispiriting.

In contrast, Libby and Erin, in strikingly similar ways, described experiences characterized by connection and joy, and this despite significant differences in their backgrounds and current lives. Before finding her current factory job, Libby had been struggling to keep mind and body together while working three low-paying jobs at the same time and raising her daughters on her own. She told of how her mother, when Libby was a teenager, had welcomed into their home a young black man who was selling encyclopedias. She told of the hours-long conversation that followed among the young man, Libby, her mother, and her brothers. Libby reported that the young man had said at one point, "I can't believe that you're actually talking to me. This is very white up here."

Erin, a medical provider,[1] told of a performance by a visiting African American "goodwill group" at her Catholic elementary school when she was in first grade. The group was composed of young children like Erin, and she remembered listening to them sing and then playing with them on the playground.

In both cases, these were stories about black visitors, strangers, coming to a "very white" place. However, both Libby and Erin claimed that these were stories of being together and close, emotionally and physically. They used words such as "bright" and "vivid" and "warm" to describe their experiences. Both claimed that they returned often to these memories.

In what follows, I attempt to make sense of what Erin and Libby told me against the backdrop of Thandeka's theorizing of white racial identity (discussed in Chapter 2) and in relation to other aspects of these women's lives. The stories that Libby and Erin told about early experiences with race did not feature the abuse described and theorized by Thandeka. Instead, desire and curiosity directed outside the white community seemed sanctioned by white authority, seemed even to be encouraged. I argue that these memories were important and were returned to, repeatedly, by Libby and Erin exactly because of white racism in their community. That is, these memories were clung to because connection and friendship and love across color lines were so rare and vulnerable in their lives.

I conclude the chapter with the story that Frank had wanted to tell me from the moment we first sat down for our interviews. In many ways, it is continuous with the racist joking in low white spaces that he described in Chapter 2. It's a story about his wife selling their van to people who Frank assumed were Mexicans living illegally in Boonendam. There are stereotypes and scapegoating. The story seems a bad fit for a chapter meant to focus on openings (even small ones) to something better. However, I argue that Frank tells the story as a joke on himself—that we can read it as Frank scapegoating himself rather than scapegoating (or only scapegoating) racial others. We can read it as Frank's halting, stumbling realization that, as a white man, he didn't know much about how to conduct himself in a world with new neighbors.

★   ★   ★

When I asked Erin about the first time she noticed she was white, she said that she knew "exactly when that was":

ERIN: We were first-graders at Blessed Virgin School and it was spring and a black group of kids came through. They were singing and they were a cultural group. We played on the playground and their hair was all Afro and curly and looked wet, and that was the first time I realized I was white. And it was so cool. We played. We were jumping rope, and hopscotch.

TIMOTHY: And they were probably Catholic kids from another place?

ERIN: Probably. They spoke English. I think they were just—

TIMOTHY: African American?

ERIN: Yup. They weren't a group coming out of Haiti or anything like that, but just a sort of goodwill group that came through the area. I don't even know who they were or what they were about, but all I know is we sang, and out on the playground, we were playing. That was it. I'll never forget it.

I am not sure why I guessed, during the interview, that these visiting black children were Catholic, other than that they had come to Erin's Catholic school. But Erin's guess that they were a "goodwill group" made sense, especially against the backdrop of what was and had been happening with race and civil rights at the time in Wisconsin and the nation.

Given her age, Erin would have been in first grade in 1967/68. There were major race riots in Detroit and Newark in the summer of 1967, and in Milwaukee (Wisconsin's largest city and one of the most segregated cities in the nation at the time), in late July, riots broke out that resulted in four deaths and 1,500 arrests. In August, the NAACP Youth Council organized a march protesting Milwaukee officials' refusal to pass an open housing ordinance. A white Catholic priest was an important part of that march and ongoing protests:

> The August 1967 march expressed the frustration of the black community but also drew the wrath of three to five thousand white residents, who shouted obscenities and threw objects at the marchers, particularly focusing

on the march's leader, Father James Groppi. Groppi, a white Catholic priest, was an important figure in the civil rights movement, playing an instrumental role in dramatizing the segregated housing situation in Milwaukee through his frequent demonstrations and arrests. Daily demonstrations continued throughout the winter of 1967–68.

(Wisconsin Historical Society, 2014)

I have not been able to confirm that the Catholic Church (or some other agency) was organizing the sorts of "goodwill" visits that Erin remembered—by black children to white communities—specifically in response to racial strife in the state. But this seems a reasonable assumption.[2]

Two other aspects of Erin's narration deserve comment here. First, Erin recognized that she was white specifically in contrast to what she perceived as the visiting children's blackness, which she said was signaled by their hair being "all Afro and curly." In other parts of this and her second interview, she would also note as differences their "black skin," their language, and their jump rope skills. Second, Erin hinted at her positive emotional response as a child to playing with and being close to these visitors—"it was so cool."

In her second interview, I asked Erin to tell me again about this experience and to talk about how it made her feel:

ERIN: I remember the [school's] old gym and the stage. I know they came in the morning because we ate lunch together. I don't remember the performance, except that some were on the stage and some were down [with us on the gym floor]. We were all on the floor in the gym, facing there and listening to it and sitting with—but the highlight of the day, the thing I can't get out of my head is that it was an absolute, bright, sunny—it had to be a spring day because it was late in the year and it was warm. It wasn't *hot* hot, but it was warm. I was in a dress and we were playing jump rope. That's all I remember, is all of the black skin, the Afros, the tight curls, and their hair looked white, especially in the sun. And their palms looked white. ... That's what I remember.

TIMOTHY: What's the emotional account of this? You tried to lay out as best you could what you remember, the events of it. So, what are you experiencing as this—

ERIN: Awe. It was really awe. It's like it was yesterday, Tim. I can see it. It's always been like that. I've always had, remembered that. It just made such an impression. I was a little one that was just in awe. It wasn't that things were different, it was just that, it was different ... I'd be fabricating things if I said I was scared. I wasn't scared. It was a very pleasant, happy—and I wasn't as competent at the jump rope as they were, so I was just impressed that they could do all these fancy things. I guess I'd be lying if I told you that this little kid, what emotions, really—but it wasn't an unhappy thing.

I cannot be certain, but I think that Erin, toward the end of this segment, made a point of saying that she "wasn't scared" because of a personal experience I had told her about earlier in the interview. I had told her about how, when I was 11 or 12 years old, I had been unable to fall asleep in a hotel when my family had stopped in Chicago as part of a family trip. I had told Erin that, as best I could figure out, I had been fearful because it seemed like the hotel was in a black neighborhood. Whether or not this is why she said this, Erin made it clear that this was a positive experience.

For Erin, one aspect of this positive experience was being *together* with these other children. She said that they ate lunch together; that they sat together on the gym floor as groups of the visiting children took turns performing on the stage and watching with Erin and her classmates; and, most importantly, that they played together, outside, in the bright, sunny, spring day.

There was a movement here, from inside to outside,[3] that seemed to contribute to the pleasure of the experience and the pleasure of remembering it (there will be a similar movement in Libby's experience, discussed below). At first, this was happening inside—inside the school, in the lunchroom, in the gym. While talking and movement were probably not as tightly controlled in the gym and lunchroom as they were in classroom spaces, I assume that these restrictions were loosened even more as the children moved outside.

For it was outside that was important: Outside was the "highlight of the day" that "made such an impression." Erin claimed to not remember anything about the performance (inside), but she remembered that outside it was bright, that it was warm, that she wore a dress (Erin said that she was very much a "tomboy" growing up and that this was not a usual thing for her), that she jumped rope with them and admired them for their skills, and that they had "black skin" and hair with "tight curls" and "palms [that] looked white."

We might worry that Erin—as a little girl and/or as a woman remembering these experiences—was relating to these black children as exotic, unusual, stimulating *objects* rather than as fellow humans (hooks, 1992). If this was part of what was happening, it seems less important than the togetherness, the physical closeness, that Erin returned to again and again and that seemed to produce the happiness and "awe" that Erin said characterized this experience.[4]

When I asked Erin what produced this "awe," she again emphasized the sense of closeness and suggested that even though they all were outside on the playground, there were still adult expectations for behavior that mattered. Here, however—and this is in almost perfect opposition to Thandeka's (2001) account of how white authority demands *separation*—Erin's attraction to these black children and an internal desire to be close seemed to align well with what she thought her white teachers wanted her to do:

> I remember the playground being packed. Feeling packed because you not only had your schoolmates there but this relatively large troupe. The swings

were full anyway but now they're really full. You wanted to share and you were told to share ... I don't know what else you want—it was just such a bright, sunny day.

White authority, here, told her to "share," but Erin suggested that she had already wanted to do this: "You wanted to share and you were told to share." In this experience, Erin did not endure feeling that her curiosity and desire to play with these black children were wrong. White adults had not only told her to share, but had sanctioned the event. And this event was characterized not only by Erin realizing that she was white/they were black, but by these differences being an occasion of pleasure and happiness for her.

★   ★   ★

Like Erin, Libby had an answer to my question about the first time she realized that she was white. In fact, she began her answer before I had even finished speaking:

TIMOTHY: I'd like you to try to think back and try to remember the first time that you noticed that you were white, or if it wasn't the first time—
LIBBY: It is so vivid in my head. I have never forgotten it. I had thought about this time and time again and probably within the last couple of months, I have. There was a college kid that came to town to sell some kind of medical encyclopedias to raise money to continue his education, and he was black. ... My mom welcomed him into the house and he sat down and we talked to him for quite a while and he said, "I can't believe that you're actually talking to me. This is very white up here." And I'm going what's that supposed to mean other than, you know, maybe skin color, and he says, "It's really refreshing." We talked to him, we all sat on the curb, my three older brothers and I sitting there, and my little brother, talking to him for hours. There were no walls. There weren't any walls there. I looked at him as another person coming through and he's a different color, but my mother was very unique meaning that she never [inaudible]. I never forgot that. Here's this guy with this big Afro and I laughed because my brother, the one they called Fuzzy, I've got pictures of him, but he let his hair go out to here. And at that time, his hair was already like—but it was funny, but "You two have the exact same hair!" And he laughed. It was our first walk into, you know, you see color on TV, but you never met anyone in person, and I didn't have a bad perception of a black person or a white person.
TIMOTHY: He obviously, by walking around town, had a different experience.
LIBBY: I do remember saying to him, "It must be very hard for you to be here without anybody of your own descent" and I think that's the way I put it. I was thinking back that that was a lot for me to say to somebody I didn't

know, and he said, "It is. I'm going to say it again—this is very white up here." I said, "Yeah."

TIMOTHY: But don't you think he was saying that he hadn't been received as well either? He wasn't just saying there were a lot of white people.

LIBBY: That's the impression I had, that he felt that nobody would talk to him, but we just invited him to come and sit down and we gave him soda or water or whatever and we talked for hours and had so much fun.

I seemed to be pushing here, at the end of this segment, for Libby to say explicitly that the young black man had experienced racial prejudice as he sold his encyclopedias around Boonendam. But it wasn't until the end that Libby admitted this, at least in her own words: "That's the impression I had, that he felt that nobody would talk to him." Before this, it was her reports of what the young man had said that, for me at least, made this crystal clear.

We might interpret Libby's reticence to label her community racist as wrapped up with a desire to think well of where she comes from. But this wasn't the case. Libby was quite explicit in other parts of her two interviews with me that she thought of the town and many of its people as racist. Indeed, she talked openly, and in strong contrast to how she described her mother, about growing up with a father she thought very prejudiced.

My hunch, then, is that what seems like Libby's reticence was actually an attempt to express, *as a narrator or author of this story,* that this was a racial awakening for her (even if she had learned about race and racism earlier in her life). As a narrator, Libby characterized her younger self as naïve, as not knowing much about race and racial prejudice. She said she "never met anyone in person, and I didn't have a bad perception of a black person or a white person." When I then suggested that the young man had experienced racism, she reported that it "was a lot" for her, at the time, to even say something to him about the lack of other people of his "descent" in the community. Of course, it was Libby as a narrator—in contrast to Libby as a character in her own story—who was in control of the image of and words spoken by herself and the young black man in the story. In the story, the young black man had knowledge and experience of race and racism; he was the one willing to say, "This is very white up here." In contrast, as a character in the story, Libby was reluctant to even say "black." (As a narrator, however, Libby had said "black" almost immediately: "There was a college kid that came to town ... and he was black.") As a character in this story, she was learning about race and being white.

There are remarkable similarities between Libby's and Erin's stories. In both, they learned that they were white in relation to black visitors and their skin and hair. In both, there was the same movement from inside to outside. In Libby's story, her mother first invited the young black man into the house, where "he sat down and we talked to him for quite a while." Then, the scene shifted to outside, to the curb in front of the house, where Libby, her brothers, and the young man talked "for hours."

As with Erin's story, it was the outside that seemed most important to Libby. What happened inside was barely treated, but Libby's description of the outside was expansive in both temporal and spatial terms. They talked "for hours and had so much fun." And Libby claimed "There were no walls. There weren't any walls there." I assume she was speaking metaphorically, but there was also a literal sense to this as they sat on the curb outside together. Libby sustained this sense of 'outside' when she used the metaphor of going for a walk—something you do outdoors—to represent learning about race and being white: "It was our first walk into, you know, you see color on TV, but you never met anyone in person."

Outside was also the site of pleasure, with "fun" in talking and sharing something to drink and with laughter caused by the juxtaposition of sameness and difference. Libby thought that her white brother, Fuzzy, had the "exact same hair" as the young black man with the Afro. She laughed. The young man laughed.

Finally, the fun and laughter, the inside and the outside of this experience, were sanctioned by white authority. It was Libby's mother who "welcomed him into the house." Later in her story (and in a number of other places in her interviews), Libby described her mother as being "very unique" in her warm and respectful response to diverse others. Libby credited her mother with teaching her the importance of relating to racial others like this young black man as "another *person* coming through."

★   ★   ★

Even as I worked with Libby's and Erin's stories and felt like I was coming to understand them in fruitful ways, I remained puzzled by how prepared they seemed to be to narrate these stories and curious about why these memories seemed so important to them.

As best I can reconstruct or remember, I did not tell Erin and Libby ahead of time that I would ask them about the first time they realized they were white. I checked the short script that I had written for myself to help me talk with people about the project and whether they might want to participate. While it is certainly possible that I said more than this to some people, my script included only the following on what we would be taking up in the interviews: "The research project is focused on what people who grew up in small towns think about race and racial issues."

Thus, I tend to take Erin and Libby at their word that these were "vivid" and "bright" memories that were "like it was yesterday" and that they returned to them "time and time again."

But why? Why were these memories so important that they were recalled, replayed, again and again? Below, I explore two aspects of their lives that might help illuminate why these memories were so significant: their relationships with their parents and their experiences at work with white co-workers.

Both Erin and Libby claimed that their mothers were crucial role models and teachers of tolerance and respect for others. Both also claimed that their fathers were not.

Libby admired her father, a truck driver, for how hard he worked, but she did not like the assumptions that he made about people of color, especially black people. According to Libby, her father assumed that black people would try to steal from him when his work took him to other cities in the United States:

> When he went to Miami, Chicago, New York, Philadelphia ... if he saw somebody standing there that was black, he'd think, "Okay, what are you going to take that's mine?" That's the way he viewed it.[5]

Libby's mother, however, would not remain silent when Libby's father expressed such views in front of their children:

> But if Dad ever made a statement, my mom would rebut it and say, "Don't you guys ever feel that way. You never judge a person by looking at them. You judge them by what they do or how they act. Or let them prove themselves."

Erin did not report any such scenes of open disagreement about race between her mother and father. She admired her mother (who was a nurse) for her kindness to others and for her compassion for those in need, but Erin often found herself in conflict with her father.

In response to a question I asked about where she thought she learned about being open to those who were different from her, Erin pointed to her mother's example and to the Catholic Church. However, in this case, she was not referring to the Catholic Church that, through Blessed Virgin School, had sponsored her joyful time with black children on the playground in first grade. This time, she was referring to a Catholic Church that she believed was too rigid and "black and white" in its rules and teachings. She was not talking about racial tolerance, specifically, here. Instead, she was saying that the Church's severity and rigidity helped her recognize the opposing value of open-mindedness. She also expressed something of her feelings toward her father:

> Catholicism enforces rules by guilt ... punishment and burning in hell for the rest of your life. Ten commandments. Honor thy father and mother. Every time you thought your father was an asshole, you were going to hell, 'cause that's what you were told ... I really never bought into the rules. It taught me tolerance but not because of the religion and the rules, but because I didn't believe them. It didn't apply to the world as I was seeing it and as it was changing. It was intolerant and that wasn't right. So, I think it had the opposite effect.

Erin was a serious athlete *and* a serious musician as she grew up. She dreamed of being the Green Bay Packers' first female quarterback, and she eventually studied music in college. As with Robert in the last chapter, her heroes were black men. In football, she loved Travis Williams, who as a rookie with the Green Bay Packers in 1967 set an NFL record by returning four kickoffs for touchdowns in a single season. In music, her idol was Miles Davis on trumpet (her instrument).

Identifying with black athletes and musicians as she did put her in conflict with her father in relation to both gender and race. When Erin wanted to go out for the high school football team, her father was adamant that she stop being a "tomboy" and "grow up":

ERIN: My father being on the school board said I couldn't. They didn't allow me to go out for football. I really wanted to go out for football. They wouldn't let me because it wasn't right back then. I never forgot that.

TIMOTHY: Did you try to do it fall of your freshman year?

ERIN: Yeah. He said, "Absolutely under no circumstances are you going to embarrass me. It's well and good that just a few number of people know that you're a tomboy, but that's where it ends. You're done. Grow up."

If this experience, among others, taught Erin that her father expected her to perform her gender in a particular way, she also knew that she was not supposed to act "black"—and in this case, it seemed that her father and mother agreed:

> When we grew up, to be like "black" was not good. My parents did not like the idea that my brother had *Bitches Brew* [a Miles Davis album], and it was during the day, when they were at work, that we were upstairs listening to it ... It was not—we did not really emulate that way, the talk, the walk. It was seen as undisciplined and rough and low.

Thus, as Erin and Libby grew up, white authority did not always act as it had when Blessed Virgin teachers encouraged Erin to share and play with the visiting black children in the bright sun; it did not always act as Libby's mom had when she welcomed into her home the young black man who talked with Libby for hours and hours. White authority, including their fathers, often acted differently. It acted as Thandeka (2001) had documented in the childhood stories of white women and men where separation from racial others and identification with whiteness (*not* blackness) were *de rigueur*.

These demands and expectations did not, of course, magically disappear when Erin and Libby grew up.[6] The second aspect of Libby's and Erin's experiences that I want to gesture toward, then, in order to understand why they held on tightly to early memories of connection and joy, are their experiences at work.

For Libby struggled with her white co-workers. At the factory where Libby worked, new Hmong American employees regularly asked for her to train them—word had spread that she, unlike others, would take the time needed to train them so they could avoid injury on the line. Libby was well aware of the racism Hmong people experienced. Furthermore, she was criticized by her white co-workers for the care that she took in training her new colleagues and for the way that she stuck up for them. Libby, like her mother, was not one to remain silent in the face of something she thought wrong:

> I was calling my own crew close-minded. I said, "How many of you watch documentaries on PBS? Africa, Asia, China, wherever?" One said, "I do." And I said, "You found it interesting, didn't you. Why don't you ask them about their culture?"

Erin, who worked in a nearby city, also ran afoul of white co-workers, but in her case it was because they questioned how trusting she was of the people of color who came to her medical clinic for care. In addition, Erin questioned herself, worrying that she profiled patients—unconsciously, racially—with consequences for their care.

Many of her patients lived in poverty and could not count on timely health care. If they complained of a toothache or back pain (diagnoses she might not be able to confirm with other available evidence), they might not be able to get an appointment with a dentist or doctor for weeks or even months, and she felt compelled to prescribe pain medication to ease their suffering. However, there had been a few cases in the area where patients had used such complaints to receive drugs that they then sold to others illegally (what Erin calls "diverting," below).

Erin worried that she made different decisions about patients and their honesty depending on their race, even as she was criticized continuously by white colleagues in her office who thought that she was too trusting of people of color. In what follows, Erin discussed racism in terms of having different embodied responses to people of different races—in this case, she talked about racism in relation to the hairs on the back of her neck standing up:

> I was thinking of racism—is that's the first hairs that go up on the back of my neck, so I'm being very critical of myself in that. Do I give the prescription? Yes ... I document, does that look too uncomfortable? As long as I don't know they're diverting, it's okay. As soon as the suspicions are high enough and I find they're diverting, then it becomes morally unethical for you to write that. ... That's not the definition of racism. Racism is the first hair on the back of your neck stands up, 20-year-old black male—not the 20-year-old white male. I thought, "you do it." That's where that profiling comes from ... I think we deal with that

subconsciously every day. I recognize it. Sometimes I don't recognize it. I'm just appalled sometimes what the staff at the clinic will say. "You're doing this for that? I wouldn't give them the time of day." So I see myself as being more tuned in and I was just sort of appalled to think that, you know, I really do have a certain amount of that going on.

Erin wanted to think of herself as someone who was "tuned in" and doing what was right—easing suffering, not profiling. She was "appalled" by how her colleagues talked and acted, but at the same time she admitted that she had different embodied responses to young men depending on whether they were black or white. She was "just sort of appalled" by the thought that her body responded this way and worried that this response influenced how she cared for her patients.

It is in relation to stories of conflict and demands for separation—stories of internal struggles with embodied responses to race; stories of clashes with white co-workers; stories of white fathers who believed that their white daughters should be suspicious of black people and never attracted to the way they moved in the world—it is against the backdrop of such stories that we should interpret Libby's and Erin's memories of connection. Erin and Libby held onto these stories as brief, rare openings to something better. These memories were warm and vivid because, unfortunately, Thandeka (2001) was right. Their stories were exceptions that proved the rule.

★   ★   ★

I suppose that I have put off sharing Frank's story about selling a van to new residents of Boonendam as long as I can. I have shared it with others before—in classes I've taught, in talks that I've given. The initial responses from listeners have always been negative.

Unfounded assumptions and stereotypes flourish in the story. As narrator, Frank assumes that everyone who speaks Spanish in Boonendam must be from Mexico. Further, he assumes that these "Mexicans" must be undocumented immigrants, whom he dehumanizes and criminalizes by calling them "illegal aliens."

As characters in Frank's story, these "Mexicans" are crafted out of durable and pervasive stereotypes of Mexican Americans in the United States.[7] The men are treacherous, hot-tempered 'bandidos.' If in William's imagination the black men always had knives, then here, in Frank's flights of fancy, these bandidos rob a bank and, at a key moment in the story, run back into their house to get a gun so they can threaten Frank with it. (Of course, we, as audience for the story, doubt that any of this true—and it isn't, but the stereotype always leads, is always first.) And *of course* there is a woman, with a baby on her hip, who suddenly transforms into an exotic Latina temptress and threatens Frank's well-being by making it so hard for him to look away—which he must if he is to avoid her bandido husband's violence.

Indeed, Frank's story is an object lesson in how stereotypes deform communication and impede learning. In their discussion of "images of the outsider" in American culture, critical race theorists Richard Delgado and Jean Stefancic (1997) worry about exactly the sort of scene that Frank describes, in which a white person with little genuine contact with Mexican Americans falls back on convenient counterfeit images for sense-making. They write:

> When such a person meets actual Mexican Americans, he or she tends to place the other in one of the ready-made categories. Stereotyping thus denies members of both groups the opportunity to interact with each other on anything like a complex, nuanced human level.
>
> *(1997, p. 175)*

This is a different analysis than Ellison's (1953/1995, 1986) of the dangers of stereotyping. And, perhaps counterintuitively, it is Ellison's analysis that I use below to redeem at least one aspect of Frank's story.

But first, Frank's story.

★   ★   ★

Same time of year, last year, we just had the city garage sale. My wife Laura wants to have a garage sale. At the same time, I had an old minivan sitting around. The transmission's out. I said, "Hey, let's put it out for about $500. Let's just try to get rid of the thing."

I didn't want the garage sale to start with. We can take it to Goodwill. We can write ourselves a receipt, deduct it from our taxes. All that stress is out of our lives and that's going to have a greater financial balance to us than the $20 and 40 hours you're going to spend on this. I made her promise that day, I said, "Listen, this is all I want out of you. Don't let anyone walk around in here, in the garage, unattended, and do not let anyone into our house." Because there are people who will scope out a house, or just say "Hey, just go on in our house" and they'll steal something or whatever … just stay out of my house. They don't have to be in my house.

She calls me about noon and she says, "Hey, there's some Mexicans here looking to buy the van."

I go, "Great! Sell it to them. Fine!"

And she goes, "They don't speak any English and I'm trying to work with them. I don't think they understand that the transmission's bad." She hangs up. She calls back. She hangs up. She calls back. They think they've brokered a deal for $400 and she's confident now they know there's something wrong with the transmission and they've called somebody else to see if they can get a new one and they're going to do the work themselves. Fantastic. Something I can't do. Great.

I said "Okay, just make sure you take care of all the details that you do when you sell a vehicle and go ahead and sell it." I hung up the phone and thought to myself, "She's busy, garage sale, people there. Is she going to know enough to take the plates off of it, because it was currently still licensed in my name? And to do the title? She's sold a lot of cars on her own before, I think she will."

I pick up the phone like 60 seconds later, if that. I said, "Just make sure before you let them go, take my plates off," because I'm starting to think in my head, undocumented, illegal aliens in my van now, because if he doesn't speak English and he's living out here in one of these farm houses, he's probably only here for a little bit. "Get my plates off, make sure he signs the title so that it's not a problem."

She goes, "Oh, he's already gone."

I said, "Oh, my God! Where does he live?"

"I don't know."

"Well, what's his name?"

"George."

"George what?"

"I don't know."

"Does he have a telephone number?"

"No."

I just sold my van, titled to me, licensed to me—it's out driving around. Who knows? Pile into somebody, go rob a bank, I don't know, but it's coming to me. So at this point, I call the police and talk to Harry and ask him, "Is this bad?"

He says, "It's not so good. You should try and get those plates back." He's like, "I'll tell you what, there's that brick house that they're redoing and I think there were some Mexicans living there at the time with the other people. Why don't you just go over there. It's probably the ones that live there. It's not like there's that many of them around to find."

So, I go over there, sure as shit my van is sitting right there in the driveway, and when I went home, I took a pair of tin snips and a screwdriver, thinking if I have any trouble, I'm just snipping them off. I walk around the van, don't see anybody and thought it would probably be nice to knock, but I think it'd just be easier if I take my plates back. So, I walk up, start unscrewing the back of the license plate and all a sudden I look up and there's some people at a garage sale and they're just staring at me. I thought, "Well, this probably looks bad." I'm dressed just like this, in the middle of the afternoon, I'm like, "Don't worry about it. I just sold him the van, just forgot my plates."

And this lady just starts shaking her head and right then Harry drives by on the road. He's looking to see if I found the van. He waves at me like this and the lady's going like this and Harry just waves at her and drives on by. She finally looks at me and goes, "That's my van!"

I take a step back, "Christ! These aren't my plates!" I'm like, "Oh my God, I'm sorry." I quick tighten it up, I get back into my car and I just leave. I'm not even going to talk to her. I just had to get out of there. It's like, oh my God, I'm going to get fired. "School Teacher Stealing License Plate!"

So, I come back here to the school trying to find out this guy's address. Jan out here [in the school office] goes, "There's some Mexicans that live across the street from us."

So I said, "Okay, I have to go out there."

And [on the phone] Laura's like, "I've got something else to tell you that happened in the meantime," and I was so short with her.

I said, "What?!"

She says, "I let somebody into the house."

I said, "I can't deal with that now," because there has to be something more to it.

She says, "Oh, you're not going to like it."

So, now it's like two in the afternoon and I drive out to an old farm and there's enough cars out there to fill a small parking lot. Drive in, get out of my car, start to walk up. There's my van. Yep, right license plate this time. Here I am with tin snips and a screwdriver. I started undoing the back plate and it's all rusted out and all of a sudden this Mexican gentleman comes out of the house speaking Spanish and I have no clue.

So, I'm working faster and he's like, "Stop, stop!"

And I said, "Don't worry!"

He's like, "Stop!"

"I'm gonna in a minute if you quit talking to me. I'm going to hurry up and get done."

I'm trying to act like I know what's going on and he walks up and kind of pushes me out of the way and he says something about his brother, the van, and "You can't be touching that."

And I'm trying to explain to him, "No, these are my plates and I need them back," and he storms back into the house and I'm thinking, "It's a gun! It's a group of them!" I don't know what it is but this isn't good, because he looked mad. Out comes the other guy. He's the guy that bought the van and we're having broken English about "I just need these plates," and the whole time we're doing it, I'm working on it. I've got the back plate off. I'm getting the front plate off. At least I get the plates. I said, "Now, I'm coming back with the title and you're going to sign it," and he's narrowly getting that, so I leave. I'm just drenched with sweat and I think, "I can't believe this is happening."

I go home. "Where's the title?" And my wife has giant rubber gloves on and I'm like, "If this has anything to do with the person being in the house, don't tell me now. Just give me the title."

"Well, it does. Here's the title."

"I can't deal with this right now. Why do you have giant rubber gloves on?"

So, I go back out there and he invites me into the house now and I'm so nervous again, but we're still pretty comfortable yet and he brings his wife out. She speaks much better English and she's bouncing the baby and has the stereotypical, what you would think the Mexican, you know, she's all ratted up with the kid, she's got this big, loose blouse on that doesn't fit her, and this big flowery skirt on. So I said, "You've got to sign here," and all this sort of stuff. He's sitting at the kitchen table. She's standing next to him.

I'm explaining to her and she's talking to him and she bends over like this to try to talk to him and it just happened to be the way I was standing there. I'm completely under stress. I look up and her blouse is like not even there. Standing there without a bra. Full, exposed breasts and I'm just like, "Oh, my God!" I look up at the ceiling, like if he didn't have a reason to kill me before. He's probably a hard-core Catholic. "Looking at my wife, you son of a bitch! First you want my plates, now you want my woman." All this stuff going through my head.

And she asks me, "What's going on?"

And I say, "Beautiful ceiling!" She stands back up. There's no way I'm telling him about this so I leave.

I'm emotionally drained. I got my plates and my title. I'm driving home and Laura calls me on the cell.

"Go pick up the kids at the elementary school."

I get to the elementary school, I walk in. Standing in the office, there's the woman who I was stealing the license plates from! She looks at me and goes, "Were you just—?"

"Yes, that was me." So, I told her the whole story and she's rolling on the ground laughing. I said, "I'm just glad I didn't try to snip them off."

She says, "That can't be real!"

I said, "Oh, it's all real."

I still have to go home and figure out what else is going on. So, I get home and my wife had let, after she sold the van, an old woman showed up and said, "I need to use the bathroom," and she looked kind of sick and she went into the house and didn't come out for a while.

So Laura went into the house and heard the most disgusting bowel noises coming from our downstairs bathroom. And the lady comes out and says, verbatim, "I'm so sorry. I'm so ashamed," and left.

Laura went to the downstairs bathroom and there was shit on the floor, on the walls, all over the carpet. It took her hours to clean it. The lady had like a blow out all over the place and she had taken toilet paper and tried to smear it around the tile to try and clean it up and gave up herself and threw it all away and that's why my wife was in these rubber gloves. She shut the garage sale down and she was going down there.

We threw out the toilet cover, the rugs. It was up underneath the vanity. It was everywhere.

I'm like, "See! You don't let people in your house!"

She was like, "I know, but she would have done it—"

"I would have rather hosed it off the concrete. It would have been an easier, cheaper prospect. Anything you sold today is just gone in cleaning agents and new rugs for the bathroom." We didn't even break even on the deal.

That's my day. I couldn't believe it. Here I was, looking at a Mexican lady's breasts, feared death, stealing license plates, and got a woman in my house pooping all over the walls! Is this an average day for a human? Can it get any worse than that? I don't know. It was exactly what happened, that whole day.

And my van's still driving around out there so I'm starting to question the mechanical problem. Was the transmission even bad?

My wife's like, "Oh, you've got a better van now."

"Yeah, but the other one I liked."

★ ★ ★

As a character in the story, Frank always seemed to assume the worst about the Mexican American characters. But in the end, the story itself, as narrated by Frank, undermined most of these assumptions and stereotypes, especially in relation to the bandido men. There was no bank robbery. There was no gun. When Frank returned to the farm with the title, he was simply invited into the house to sort things through with a husband and wife at the kitchen table. These people were not "only here for a little bit," as Frank had predicted, but lived in the community, so when Frank was telling the story to me a year after this happened, he said that he saw his van "still driving around out there."

Furthermore, none of the other white characters in the story seemed quite as worked up about the "Mexicans" as Frank was. The sheriff confirmed that Frank should get his license plates off the van, but certainly didn't seem to assume that these were criminals or dangerous people with whom Frank was dealing: "There's that brick house that they're redoing and I think there were some Mexicans living there at the time with the other people. Why don't you just go over there." I am not certain what the sheriff meant by "some Mexicans living there at the time with the other people," but I think he was saying that Mexican Americans and white people were living together in "that brick house"—and this sense of Mexican Americans as *both* marked as different by white people in Boonendam (still referred to as "Mexicans") *and* a familiar part of everyday life was consistent throughout the rest of the story.[8] Only Frank seemed so nervous.

Of course, our sense of Frank—as frustrated, fearful, frantic—is an effect of Frank's narration. What we know of other characters and what happened is also dependent on Frank as narrator. Within the story, Frank's character claimed, "Oh, it's all real," but Frank also told me that he had told this story many times, that he was "famous" for it. Thus, when he told me this story at the end of our second interview, he was taking up the role of a storyteller. Through repeated tellings, he had, to an extent to which we have no real access, crafted this as a story.

For me, Frank's story is crafted, is constructed, to make Frank into a bumbling, sweating fool. When he first tries to unscrew his license plates, it's the wrong van—he waves blithely to the sheriff who happens to be driving by, who waves to the woman who owns the van Frank is struggling behind; and when Frank finally discovers his mistake, he retreats in shame, with an imagined news report sounding in his ears: "School Teacher Stealing License Plate!"

When Frank finds his van at the old farm, he can't get the rusted back plate off fast enough and struggles to explain to a "Mexican gentleman," and then another, why he is trespassing and messing with a van that isn't his anymore. He fears they will do violence to him. Of course they don't, but by the time he leaves, he is "drenched with sweat."

Frank has to rush back to the farm with the title, but before he does, he (as the narrator) provides us with some ominous foreshadowing. Laura had told Frank on the phone that she, against his wishes, had let somebody into the house during the garage sale, and now as Frank grabs the title, he notices that she has on "giant rubber gloves" (end of foreshadowing).

Then, in quick succession, Frank tries not to look at a woman's breasts (afterward, he was "emotionally drained"); he has to face, at his children's elementary school, the woman whose van he mistook for the one he used to own (she laughed heartily at him); and he learns that his wife's garage sale got shut down by an old woman who abused their downstairs bathroom. (I confess that I laughed, loudly, almost barking, when Frank claimed that the old woman said, upon leaving the bathroom, "I'm so sorry. I'm so ashamed.")

The final insult to Frank is provided in a small coda at the end of the story. We learn that Frank now wonders if there ever really was anything wrong with the van, if he was mistaken even about that. He wishes it was still his, rather than the "better van" he has now and doesn't like.

As a character in his own story, Frank was the butt of the joke, a fool. More importantly, I think that Frank was figured as a *white* fool who didn't know what he needed to know in order to move smoothly in an increasingly diverse world. I did not ask people to identify themselves politically in the interviews, and Frank never said explicitly that he identified as conservative. However, the positions he staked out and comments he made suggested that he was. Frank told me that he listened to Rush Limbaugh, and in the story, it was almost as if Frank *was* Rush Limbaugh—except that this time, instead of mocking and hating everyone who was different from him, Limbaugh laughed at himself.

The laughter here does not sound like the snide snickering for which Limbaugh is famous. The story foregrounds bodies, *comic bodies*, that shit and arouse and sweat and fumble. The laughter in Frank's story sounds more like what Mikhail Bakhtin (1984) calls the laughter of the folk—a laughter with possibilities for regeneration and renewal, a laughter that understands that things change. Put another way, conservative discourse in this country has persuaded many white men, against all evidence, that they, as *white* men, are under siege in the United States and disadvantaged by contemporary law and custom. Frank appropriated this discourse and turned it on its head. For Frank *was* under siege in his story, but it turns out that this was all in his head and heart, that the trouble was caused not by his new neighbors, but by his own stereotyping and projection. One moral of Frank's story, then, is that white men have some things to learn and that instead of being angry about it, instead of whining or being hateful, we might try laughing at ourselves as we stumble our way into new ways of being.

In previous chapters, I have drawn on Ellison's writings to make sense of stereotypes and other scapegoating rituals. A nagging problem for Ellison was that he thought that scapegoating rites might be unavoidable, necessary even, for the creation of human identity. Thus, he was anxious to discover and name symbolic rites that were compatible with a democratic project. In other words, Ellison was interested in finding scapegoating rituals that served an identity-creation function without killing people or 'othering' them the way that, for example, Frank's friend did when he made fun of Hmong Americans during the basement poker game.

This led Ellison to examine humor and the blues. Taking his cue from Freud that any joke involved at least three elements or roles—a joke had a teller, had a target or butt of the joke, and had an audience—Ellison was interested in jokes that might involve the teller as also the butt and audience of the joke. That is, Ellison was interested in scapegoating rituals in which the one doing the scapegoating (the teller of the joke) might be scapegoating himself (be the butt of the joke) as well as benefiting from the scapegoating (as the audience).

Ellison thought that the blues was just this sort of joke—a blending of tragedy and comedy that allowed an individual to play and benefit from multiple roles in the joke. Philosopher Beth Eddy sums up Ellison's analysis of the blues helpfully on this point:

> The blues allows the artist to play all three human roles in the joke. By singing—by telling the joke—a person plays the expressive role and thereby participates in the role of victimization; by experiencing the pain, the person plays the butt of the joke and the victim of the sacrifice who undergoes loss; by laughing, the person receives the catharsis needed to keep going.
>
> *(2003, pp. 153–154)*

This, in the end, is my reading of Frank's story about selling a van to his new neighbors: Frank scapegoated himself. He was telling a story in which he was also the butt of the joke. And in a significant sense, he was laughing at himself as part of an effort to "keep going." Frank was singing the blues.

Frank was singing the blues, a blues born of the death of his innocence as he witnessed his uncle's hypocrisy, saw him charge people of color with not living up to standards of conduct that Norman himself continuously violated. This was the pathetic American joke for Ellison, that white Americans made people of color into scapegoats for their own fears and failings. Norman helped Frank understand this joke, and Frank sang the blues.

Frank wished that his children might grow up to be less fearful, grow up to be braver in situations where the content of their character, as white people within our racist society, was at stake. We can wish that Frank was braver—like Stan was when he defended his sister's relationship with one Mexican American man and fired a white employee for harassing another; like Erin was when she tried to come to grips with racial profiling in her own medical practice; like Libby was when she defied white co-workers and took care in training her new Hmong American colleagues on the factory line—but he wasn't.

I am trying to hold on to a small difference between Frank's story and all the others told in the basement, but maybe I shouldn't. I am trying to see if Frank's story might be read as a slight disruption of our long history of racist jokes, blackface minstrelsy shows, and stereotypical portrayals of people of color in radio, film, and TV that have contributed to the creation our society from the beginning. So—no bravery, but perhaps some possibility, some chance for growth.

Ellison thought that the blues helped people keep going. Obviously, the struggle to keep going is different for people of color and white people. As I write this in the summer of 2015, there is news that nine African American people, as they studied the Bible in their church in Charleston, South Carolina, have been killed by a white gunman who hoped to incite a race war. The news is horrific, horrific in itself and horrific in its repetition of news from Sanford, Florida, news from Staten Island, New York, news from Ferguson, Missouri, news from Cleveland, Ohio, news from Baltimore, Maryland—all news that isn't new in our country.

Obviously, the struggle to keep going is different for white folk, but Eddy (2003), in her reading of Ellison's work, suggests that white people might also sing the blues: "Through the blues, African Americans (and, in due time, perhaps all Americans willing or forced to undergo painful initiation into the American joke) can both express their agony and shore up their sense of possibility" (p. 153).

Suspended between and hiding in both high and low white spaces, Frank sang the blues.

★　　★　　★

This is an optimistic reading of Frank's story. Other ones are possible, necessary. As disturbing as the racist stereotypes and assumptions is the presence of another scapegoat in the story that I have thus far ignored: women. For it is women, not

"Mexican" men, who do the real damage in the story, who threaten Frank's property and person. His wife wanted to have the garage sale, forgot to transfer the title, and let someone in the house; the 'Mexican temptress' endangered him with her exotic body; the old white woman wrecked his bathroom. We would do well to remember what Ruth Frankenberg (1993) said about the complexity of whiteness and white racial identity:

> A range of practices, symbols, and icons have been drawn from elsewhere into the cultural practices of white people. Nor is white culture (in fact, culture in general) a material and discursive space produced and reproduced in a vacuum. Whiteness is inflected by nationhood ... [and] whiteness, masculinity, and femininity are coproducers of one another, in ways that are, in their turn, crosscut by class and by the histories of racism and colonialism.
>
> *(1993, p. 233)*

★   ★   ★

The drama's done. I have labored to be a different sort of storyteller than the one I was when I told a Brer Rabbit story in a hot high school auditorium. With the help of Delores, Frank, Erin, Robert, William, Libby, and Stan, I have tried to step forward from the wreck and death that is whiteness with a different story that might help us know ourselves better, help us understand some of the infinity of traces that create and distort who we are.

We white people are racist, down deep. But the deep down is neither monologic nor finished.

Notes

1   Erin and I decided on "medical provider" as how to name her job because, in this small community, a more precise description would have made it very difficult to mask her identity.

2   And also "reasonable" within the terms of whiteness and white racism—if these little black children were sent out to white communities to solve race problems in the state, then once again, people of color were being positioned as the ones *with a race and with responsibility for solving race problems*, while white people were positioned as without a race and without problems associated with having one. See Dyer (1997) for an exploration of this logic.

3   This movement might also be characterized as from darkness (inside) to light (outside) given that Erin linked the "highlight of the day" to the fact that it was "an absolute, bright, sunny" day.

4   I am probably not making enough of Erin's use of the word "awe" and her saying that "I was a little one that was just in awe." It is possible that she calls herself a "little one" only to indicate that she was in first grade and/or physically little, but the word "awe"

suggests that she might also be trying to express that she was small in comparison to something huge, something awe-full. I cannot help but think of how Ellison (1953/1995) argues that one of the incongruous consequences of white people's continuous scapegoating of racial others is that these others—who are constructed as 'outside' by these rituals—end up sitting right at the center of the unfolding American drama. It is possible that Erin, with the use of "awe," was signaling (as a grown-up woman narrating this, but perhaps she sensed this even as a little girl) that she was in the presence of the awe-full and awful spectacle and mystery of race in our country.

5   Libby's father seemed to imagine himself as in the same struggle with black men, over scarce resources, that William did—see Chapter 3.

6   See Deliovsky (2010) for a careful working-through of ways that white women are disciplined and punished so that they do not seek friendship and love outside the white community, as well as for her helpful discussion of whiteness as, at base, a male category.

7   Of course, I also do not know who these people were. For the purpose of interpreting Frank's story, I assume that the people he interacted with were Mexican American, primarily because Frank assumed that they were (with attendant stereotypes in play).

8   For example, Jan, who worked in the high school office, told Frank that there are "some Mexicans that live across the street from us." And it turns out that the sheriff was wrong about where Frank might find his van and that it was a white woman's van that was parked where the sheriff said "Mexicans" were living. As regards the sheriff—I should note the privilege that Frank assumed and enjoyed here in just calling up the sheriff as he did. It seems unlikely that his Mexican American neighbors would have this privilege.

THE AFTERTHOUGHT

It feels late.

★　　★　　★

During the time of the Seventh Fire, the Light-skinned Race is given a choice of two roads. One road is a slower path. On it, the Light-skinned Race joins the New People of the Ojibwe who have learned with their elders and have recovered—as Edward Benton-Banai (1988), author of *The Mishomis Book: The Voice of the Ojibway*, writes—"what was left by the trail" (pp. 92–93). On this slower path, the "Earth is not scorched" and the "grass is still growing there" (p. 93).

During the time of the Seventh Fire, the Light-skinned Race is given a choice of two roads. On the second, the Light-skinned Race continues to wear the face of death and the "destruction they brought with them in coming to this country will come back to them and cause much suffering and death to all the Earth's people" (p. 93).

★　　★　　★

They were waiting for the dove to come back.

The Creator, Adonai, had flooded the entire Earth. Noah and his family and the animals waited in a giant ark. The dove returned with an olive leaf in its mouth, the water receded, and eventually the people and animals inhabited all the Earth.

And like Moses and the children of Israel in Egypt, the enslaved Africans in America prayed to God and shook off the chains of bondage, only to endure lynchings and Jim Crow and mass incarceration and racist representation, seemingly without end—all taken up, all reinforced from below, by white folk who should have been their neighbors, their comrades, their fellow citizens, their brothers and sisters.

In the midst of the ongoing struggle, James Baldwin beseeched white folk to finally come to understand themselves, to learn to love themselves, so that we could finally walk arm in arm with black folk:

> I do not know many Negroes who are eager to be "accepted" by white people, still less to be loved by them; they, the blacks, simply don't wish to be beaten over the head by the whites every instant of our brief passage on this planet. White people in this country will have quite enough to do in learning how to accept and love themselves and each other, and when they have achieved this—which will not be tomorrow and may very well be never—the Negro problem will no longer exist, for it will no longer be needed.
>
> *(1963/1993, pp. 21–22)*

Baldwin prophesized that if we finally came to understand ourselves and, with black folk, "do not falter in our duty," we may be able to act together to "end the racial nightmare, and achieve our country, and change the history of the world" (p. 105).

As in the Seventh Fire, however, white folk have a choice. We can continue on the path of ignorance and destruction we have been walking. If we do, then we are lost.

And there will be no rainbow, as with Noah and his descendants, to reassure us. There will be—*listen* to Baldwin singing a sorrow song created by his ancestors in the depths of slavery—there will be no water, either. Just fire. Just "the fire next time" (p. 106).

★   ★   ★

It's late.

METHODOLOGICAL APPENDIX

> The youth gets together his materials to build a bridge to the moon ... and at
> length the middle-aged man concludes to build a wood-shed with them.
> — *Thoreau*

Delores, Frank, William, Robert, Stan, Erin, and Libby were part of a larger
interview study of race and whiteness in Boonendam. The study, grounded in
interpretive research methods and assumptions (see especially Erickson, 1986),
involved open-ended, in-depth interviews with 22 participants. These participants
represented roughly three generations of white people living in this rural
community—generations that grew up before, during, and after the civil rights
movement. At the time of the interviews, participants ranged in age from 18 to
83 years of age, included equal numbers of women and men, and included people
pursuing (and retired from) a range of occupations, including farmer, factory and
office worker, student, and educator. Initial interviews lasted one to three hours;
follow-up interviews were one to two hours long. Interview questions explored
the meaning of whiteness for participants and how the meaning of whiteness
changed over time, within lifetimes, and from generation to generation. The
interviews were audiotaped and transcribed. Transcripts were analyzed using
inductive methods (Erickson, 1986; Glaser and Strauss, 1967; Hammersly and
Atkinson, 1983).

Drawing on a series of his own interview studies, Eduardo Bonilla-Silva (2001,
2003; Bonilla-Silva and Forman, 2000) has challenged the findings of large-scale
surveys that suggest that white people's attitudes toward people of color have
improved in the United States since the civil rights era. Bonilla-Silva argues that,

instead, what has changed is *white discourse about race*, with white people avoiding racist talk and embracing a language of color-blindness.

As I initially conceptualized my study, I was curious if differences in white talk would surface among older and younger white people. Early analyses of the interviews, however, did not expose significant differences across generations in the talk used by participants. Old as well as young avoided racist terminology. There also was little of the "incoherent talk," the "slippery, apparently contradictory, and often subtle" language that Bonilla-Silva (2003, p. 53) documented. I suspect that at least part of the contrast in white talk across our studies has to do with contrasting interview questions and schedules.

Bonilla-Silva's research teams asked direct questions about affirmative action, interracial dating and marriage, and societal inequality. My interviews were less structured and began with questions about participants' experiences with (or stories that they had heard about) conflicts between the German and, later, Polish immigrants who settled this community. (German immigrants began settling in the area in the late 1850s, with Polish immigrants starting to arrive about two decades later.) This part of the interview was informed by Matthew Jacobson's (1998) historical account of the hierarchies and struggles among different white ethnic groups in the United States, well into the twentieth century, as to who were superior white people and who were not.

Then, inspired by Thandeka's (2001) work, I asked participants to try to remember the first time that they noticed they were white and to narrate experiences in which being white somehow mattered or was important. From there, we moved on to explorations of how they and their community had interacted with or responded to people of color in various situations and across different historical events, including: 1) the relatively recent practice of hiring Hmong and Mexican American immigrants to work on local farms, and 2) the controversy surrounding Ojibwe efforts in the 1970s to claim their fishing rights, guaranteed by nineteenth-century federal treaties with the U.S. government, on nearby lakes and rivers (Loew, 2001).

As my work with the interviews progressed, I became less interested in questions of how the meaning of whiteness changed for individuals or of differences in white talk across generations and more interested in how participants' sense of themselves as white people was connected to experiences with people of color (real or imagined). I realized that one of the unexamined assumptions I had brought to this research was that, since participants led largely segregated lives, people of color would have little to do with their social and psychic lives. In other words, I had assumed that my data analysis would expose *isolation* from people of color, rather than *relation or connection*, as undergirding the production of white racial indentities.

As an educator and teacher educator, I was attracted to Delores's stories about studying to be a teacher during the late 1960s, and from my current vantage point, I can say that my work on *White Folks* began when I settled into figuring out what was going on in Delores's interviews. Eventually, I finished a paper on Delores and moved on to Frank's interviews—and by the time I had finished a long paper on Frank, I had abandoned the idea of trying to write about three generations of white people in Boonendam.

Partly, this was because I work and write slowly—simple math told me that for any foreseeable future I would be working with only a subset of the interviews. More importantly, I was becoming clearer about two important commitments that I brought to the writing of *White Folks*.

The first was that I wanted to find a way to write in which I did not, as author, separate myself from or suggest that I was superior to the people I was writing about. I worried that it would be too easy to write about white people a generation older and younger than me as *different* from me—which I didn't want to do. Too much writing on race and whiteness by white authors has these authors separating themselves from their subjects, usually by making it clear that the authors are *good* white people in contrast to the bad ones written about. If these authors tell stories about themselves, they often achieve a similar discontinuity by telling redemption stories—once I was lost (like other bad white people), but now I am found (to be a good white person). Although it is not the only place in the book where I attempt to perform continuity rather than discontinuity, the autoethnographic first chapter of *White Folks* is certainly meant to make plain that I am caught up in the same processes of white racial identity creation as Delores and the rest.

However, even as I worked to not separate myself, in my writing, from the research participants, I also did not want to suggest that our thoughts, feelings, and lives were the same. We were varied, multiple: different from each other and multiple, conflicted, within ourselves.

Representing this variation is important because the current dominant critical framework for understanding whiteness—a *white privilege* framework, popularized by writers such as Peggy McIntosh (1988) and Tim Wise (2008)—tends to conceptualize white people as little more than the smooth embodiment of racism and white privilege. Increasingly, antiracist researchers and educators have argued that this framework has undermined, rather than strengthened, antiracist efforts and that alternative renderings of whiteness and white racial identity are needed (Conklin, 2008; Jupp et al., 2016; Lensmire et al., 2013; Lowenstein, 2009; McCarthy, 2003; Thandeka, 2001; Trainor, 2002; Winans, 2005). Toward this end, James Jupp and Patrick Slattery (2010) called for a "second wave" of white identity studies—a second wave meant to supersede a first one that was too often reductive, that too often insisted that "Whites de facto represent a static, monolithic, and ontological White supremacist homeland. What a tragic error, we think, to emphasize essentializing stasis, if that is what, in fact, we seek to change" (p. 471)

The second important commitment I brought to my writing, then, was to represent complexities and conflicts at the heart of white racial selves. In this, I was guided not only by criticism of past research and by what I was seeing in the interviews, but also by Ellison's (1953/1995) writing on how black people have too often been simplified and stereotyped in American literature. I do not invoke Ellison here to suggest that white folk have suffered anything like the magnitude of symbolic violence directed at black people. However, within antiracist writing and teaching, there has been an unhelpful simplification of who white people are, and I have looked to Ellison for direction on how to pursue, in my writing, something different. Here is an example of how Ellison framed his critique and his image of something better:

> Too often what is presented as the American Negro (a most complex example of Western man) emerges an oversimplified clown, a beast or an angel. Seldom is he drawn as that sensitively focused process of opposites, of good and evil, of instinct and intellect, of passion and spirituality, which great literary art has projected as the image of man.
>
> *(1953/1995, pp. 25–26)*

My purposes and accomplishments are obviously humbler than great literary art, but Ellison's call—an ethical demand, really—for representations of humans as "sensitively focused process[es] of opposites" is one I have tried to answer.

Of course, I have needed to respond to other ethical demands throughout the research and writing. I have used pseudonyms for places and people, but since some people know (including people from Boonendam) where I grew up, I have had to take special care with masking the identities of participants. Interviews were conducted in people's homes, offices, private rooms—for the few that weren't, we sat and talked in a coffee shop with the small electronic device that I used to record the interviews on the table, close to the participant; we saw no one we knew during these interviews. I discussed and arranged with participants how to both describe and obscure important aspects of their lives. For example, I have used only "educator" or "teacher" for people who took up a range of more specific positions within different sorts of schools. In these discussions with participants, I was usually much more intent than they were about figuring out how to protect their confidentiality. Over and over, they expressed that they felt they should be willing to stand by, take responsibility for, what they said. I told them that I appreciated this sentiment—and that I would ignore its implication and work hard to mask who they were.

However, I must embrace this sentiment in relation to my book. In *White Folks*, I have positioned myself, have figured myself, as a storyteller, and in this role I have not only told stories about my own experiences, but also appropriated the stories of others. In the interviews, we often tried, together, to make sense of what the participants were telling me. We often made their own stories the objects of mutual exploration and discussion. But in the end, I have selected the stories to retell; and I have interpreted and theorized what they meant.

I have also appropriated stories from other writers. Perhaps the appropriation that feels the most fraught to me is my use of Ojibwe stories in my forethought and afterthought. Within the body of the book, I spend a fair amount of time criticizing how white people have appropriated the stories and cultures of racial others. I know that good intentions—I used these stories to begin the story of Boonendam not with white settlers, but with those whose sovereignty had been trampled—are never enough.

I made up the name for Boonendam from the Ojibwe word *boonenim*, which means to quit thinking or worrying about; to forget, ignore. Unlike the sorts of appropriation found in blackface minstrelsy—where black ways of moving in the world were distorted and mocked so white folk could forget who they were, could quit thinking or worrying about where they were in society and history—I used (and tried to take care with) these Ojibwe stories so that white folk will not forget who and where we are.

REFERENCES

Alexander, M. (2010). *The new Jim Crow: Mass incarceration in the age of colorblindness.* New York: New Press.

Allen, T. (2012). *The invention of the white race, vol. 2: The origin of racial oppression in Anglo-America.* Brooklyn, NY: Verso.

Bakhtin, M.M. (1984). *Rabelais and his world.* (H. Iswolsky, Trans.). Bloomington: Indiana University.

Baldwin, J. (1993). *The fire next time.* New York: Vintage International. (Original work published 1963)

Benton-Banai, E. (1988). *The Mishomis book: The voice of the Ojibway.* Hayward, WI: Indian Country Communications.

Blobaum, D. (2008). A chronology, *Chicago '68.* Retrieved November 23, 2016, from www.chicago68.com/c68chron.html

Bonilla-Silva, E. (2001). *White supremacy and racism in the post-civil rights era.* Boulder, CO: Lynne Rienner.

Bonilla-Silva, E. (2003). *Racism without racists: Color-blind racism and the persistence of racial inequality in the United States.* Lanham, MD: Rowman & Littlefield.

Bonilla-Silva, E., and Forman, T. (2000). "I am not a racist but ...": Mapping White college students' racial ideology in the USA. *Discourse & Society, 11*(1), 50–85.

Boskin, J. (1986). *Sambo: The rise and demise of an American jester.* New York: Oxford University Press.

Brasch, W. (2000). *Brer Rabbit, Uncle Remus, and the "Cornfield Journalist": The tale of Joel Chandler Harris.* Macon, GA: Mercer University Press.

Brown, S. (1933). Negro character as seen by white authors. *Journal of Negro Education, 2*(2), 179–203.

Cockrell, D. (1997). *Demons of disorder: Early blackface minstrels and their world.* New York: Cambridge University Press.

Conklin, H. (2008). Modeling compassion in critical, justice-oriented teacher education. *Harvard Educational Review, 78*(4), 652–674.

Cosby, B., and Poussaint, A. (2007). *Come on, people: On the path from victims to victors.* Nashville, TN: Thomas Nelson.

Delgado, R., and Stefancic, J. (1997). Images of the outsider in American law and culture. In R. Delgado and J. Stefancic (Eds.), *Critical white studies: Looking behind the mirror* (pp. 170–178). Philadelphia, PA: Temple University Press.

Deliovsky, K. (2010). *White femininity: Race, gender and power.* Halifax and Winnipeg: Fernwood Publishing.

Deloria, P. (1998). *Playing Indian.* New Haven, CT: Yale University Press.

Dewey, J. (1966). *Democracy and education.* New York: Free Press. (Original work published 1916)

Dixon Gottschild, B. (1996). *Digging the Africanist presence in American performance: Dance and other contexts.* Westport, CT: Greenwood Press.

Du Bois, W.E.B. (1992). *Black reconstruction in America.* New York: The Free Press. (Original work published 1935)

Du Bois, W. E. B. (1997). *The souls of black folk.* Boston, MA: Bedford Books. (Original work published 1903)

Dyer, R. (1997). *White.* New York: Routledge.

Eddy, B. (2003). *The rites of identity: The religious naturalism and cultural criticism of Kenneth Burke and Ralph Ellison.* Princeton, NJ: Princeton University.

Ellison, R. (1986). *Going to the territory.* New York: Vintage International.

Ellison, R. (1995). *Shadow and act.* New York: Vintage International. (Original work published 1953)

Emerson, K. (1997). *Doo-dah! Stephen Foster and the rise of American popular culture.* New York: Simon & Schuster.

Erickson, F. (1986). Qualitative methods in research on teaching. In M.C. Wittrock (Ed.), *Handbook on research on teaching* (3rd ed., pp. 119–161). New York: MacMillan.

Fairclough, N. (2003). "Political correctness": The politics of culture and language. *Discourse & Society, 14*(1), 17–28.

Fedo, M. (2000). *The lynchings in Duluth.* St. Paul, MN: Minnesota Historical Society Press.

Fiedler, L. (1955). *An end of innocence.* Boston, MA: Beacon.

Fiedler, L. (1964). *Waiting for the end.* New York: Stein and Day.

Frankenberg, R. (1993). *White women, race matters: The social construction of whiteness.* Minneapolis, MN: University of Minnesota.

Frost, L. (2005). *Never one nation: Freaks, savages, and whiteness in U.S. popular culture, 1850–1877.* Minneapolis, MN: University of Minnesota.

Glaser, B., and Strauss, A.L. (1967). *The discovery of grounded theory: Strategies for qualitative research.* Chicago: Aldine.

Gooding-Williams, R. (1993). *Reading Rodney King: Reading urban uprising.* New York: Routledge.

Gramsci, A. (1971). *Selections from the Prison Notebooks.* New York: International Publishers.

Guinier, L., and Torres, G. (2002). *The miner's canary: Enlisting race, resisting power, transforming democracy.* Cambridge, MA: Harvard University Press.

Hammersly, M., and Atkinson, P. (1983). *Ethnography: Principles in practice.* London: Tavistock.

Harris, J.C. (1911). *Uncle Remus, his songs and his sayings.* New York: D. Appleton.

hooks, b. (1992). *Black looks: Race and representation.* Cambridge, MA: South End Press.

Jacobson, M. (1998). *Whiteness of a different color: European immigrants and the alchemy of race.* Cambridge, MA: Harvard University Press.

Jones Royster, J. (Ed.) (1997). *Southern horrors and other writings: The anti-lynching campaign of Ida B. Wells, 1892–1900.* Boston, MA: Bedford Books.

Jupp, J., and Slattery, P. (2010). Committed white male teachers and identifications: Toward creative identifications and a "second wave" of white identity studies. *Curriculum Inquiry, 40*(3), 454–474.

Jupp, J., Berry, T., and Lensmire, T. (2016). Second-wave white teacher identity studies: A review of white teacher identity literatures from 2004 through 2014. *Review of Educational Research, 86*(4), 1151–1191. DOI: 10.3102/0034654316629798

Kovol, J. (1970). *White racism: A psychohistory.* New York: Pantheon.

Lensmire, T., and Snaza, N. (2010). What teacher education can learn from blackface minstrelsy. *Educational Researcher, 39*(5), 413–422.

Lensmire, T., McManimon, S., Dockter Tierney, J., Lee-Nichols, M., Casey, Z., Lensmire, A., and Davis, B. (2013). McIntosh as synecdoche: How teacher education's focus on white privilege undermines antiracism. *Harvard Educational Review, 83*(3), 410–431.

Lhamon, W.T. (1998). *Raising Cain: Blackface performance from Jim Crow to hip hop.* Cambridge, MA: Harvard University Press.

Lhamon, W.T. (2003). *Jump Jim Crow: Lost plays, lyrics, and street prose of the first Atlantic popular culture.* Cambridge, MA: Harvard University Press.

Loew, P. (2001). *Indian nations of Wisconsin: Histories of endurance and renewal.* Madison, WI: Wisconsin Historical Society Press.

Lott, E. (1995). *Love and theft: Blackface minstrelsy and the American working class.* New York: Oxford University Press.

Lowenstein, K. (2009). The work of multicultural teacher education: Reconceptualizing white teacher candidates as learners. *Review of Educational Research, 79*(1), 163–196.

McCarthy, C. (2003). Contradictions of power and identity: Whiteness studies and the call of teacher education. *Qualitative Studies in Education, 16*(1), 127–133.

McIntosh, P. (1988). *White privilege and male privilege: A personal account of coming to see correspondences through work in women's studies* (Working Paper 189). Wellesley, MA: Wellesley Center for Research on Women.

Mailer, N. (1959). *Advertisements for myself.* New York: G.P. Putnam's Sons.

Media Education Foundation. (1997). Stuart Hall: Race, the floating signifier, *Media Education Foundation.* Retrieved December 11, 2012, from www.mediaed.org/cgi-bin/commerce.cgi?preadd =action&key=407

Melville, H. (1949) *Moby Dick.* Garden City, NY: Nelson Doubleday. (Original work published in 1851)

Morrison, T. (1989). Unspeakable things unspoken: The Afro-American presence in American literature. *Michigan Quarterly Review, 28*(1), 1–34.

Morrison, T. (1992). *Playing in the dark: Whiteness and the literary imagination.* Cambridge, MA: Harvard University Press.

Roediger, D. (1991). *The wages of whiteness.* London: Verso.

Schick, C., and St. Denis, V. (2005). Troubling national discourses in anti-racist curricular planning. *Canadian Journal of Education, 28*(3), 295–317.

Srivastava, S. (2005). "You're calling me a racist?" The moral and emotional regulation of antiracism and Feminism. *Signs: Journal of Women in Culture and Society, 31*(1), 29–62.

Thandeka. (2001). *Learning to be white: Money, race, and God in America*. New York: Continuum.

Trainor, J. (2002). Critical pedagogy's "other": Constructions of whiteness in education for social change. *College Composition and Communication, 53*(4), 631–650.

Twain, M. (1962). *The adventures of Huckleberry Finn*. New York: Airmont. (Original work published 1885)

Walt Disney Presents. (1974). *Walt Disney's Uncle Remus*. Racine, WI: Golden Press.

Waziyatawin. (2008). *What does justice look like? The struggle for liberation in Dakota homeland*. St. Paul, MN: Living Justice Press.

Winans, A. (2005). Local pedagogies and race: Interrogating white safety in the rural college classroom. *College English, 67*(3), 253–273.

Wisconsin Historical Society. (2014). Desegregation and civil rights, *Wisconsin Historical Society*. Retrieved 16 February, 2016, from www.wisconsinhistory.org/turningpoints/tp-049/?action=more_essay

Wise, T. (2008). *White like me: Reflections on race from a privileged son*. Berkeley, CA: Soft Skull Press.

Wolfe, B. (1949). Uncle Remus and the malevolent rabbit. *Commentary, 8*, 31–41.

Woods II, L.L. (2015). Killing for inclusion: Racial violence and assimilation into the whiteness gang. In E. Harris and A. Tillis (Eds.), *The Trayvon Martin in US: An American tragedy* (pp. 113–124). New York: Peter Lang.

INDEX

Taylor & Francis eBooks

Helping you to choose the right eBooks for your Library

Add Routledge titles to your library's digital collection today. Taylor and Francis ebooks contains over 50,000 titles in the Humanities, Social Sciences, Behavioural Sciences, Built Environment and Law.

Choose from a range of subject packages or create your own!

Benefits for you

>> Free MARC records
>> COUNTER-compliant usage statistics
>> Flexible purchase and pricing options
>> All titles DRM-free.

REQUEST YOUR **FREE** INSTITUTIONAL TRIAL TODAY

Free Trials Available
We offer free trials to qualifying academic, corporate and government customers.

Benefits for your user

>> Off-site, anytime access via Athens or referring URL
>> Print or copy pages or chapters
>> Full content search
>> Bookmark, highlight and annotate text
>> Access to thousands of pages of quality research at the click of a button.

eCollections – Choose from over 30 subject eCollections, including:

Archaeology	Language Learning
Architecture	Law
Asian Studies	Literature
Business & Management	Media & Communication
Classical Studies	Middle East Studies
Construction	Music
Creative & Media Arts	Philosophy
Criminology & Criminal Justice	Planning
Economics	Politics
Education	Psychology & Mental Health
Energy	Religion
Engineering	Security
English Language & Linguistics	Social Work
Environment & Sustainability	Sociology
Geography	Sport
Health Studies	Theatre & Performance
History	Tourism, Hospitality & Events

For more information, pricing enquiries or to order a free trial, please contact your local sales team:
www.tandfebooks.com/page/sales

Routledge
Taylor & Francis Group

The home of
Routledge books

www.tandfebooks.com